THE SIPSTER'S POCKET GUIDE
TO 50 MUST-TRY ONTARIO WINES

VOLUME 1

VOL.
1

THE
Sipster's
POCKET GUIDE
TO 50 MUST-TRY
ONTARIO WINES

LUKE WHITTALL

TOUCHWOOD

TouchWood Editions
touchwoodeditions.com

The information in this book is true and complete to the best
of the author's knowledge. All recommendations are made
without guarantee on the part of the author or the publisher.

Copy edited by Senica Maltese
Cover and interior design by Sydney Barnes
Typeset by Sara Loos
Photography by Luke Whittall,
with the following exceptions: pages 20, 32, 82, 86, 90, 94,
and 98 (courtesy of the wineries)

CATALOGUING DATA AVAILABLE FROM LIBRARY AND ARCHIVES CANADA
ISBN 9781771514217 (softcover)
ISBN 9781771514224 (electronic)

TouchWood Editions acknowledges that the land on which
we live and work is within the traditional territories of the
Lkwungen (Esquimalt and Songhees), Malahat, Pacheedaht,
Scia'new, T'Sou-ke and W̱SÁNEĆ (Pauquachin, Tsartlip,
Tsawout, Tseycum) peoples.

We acknowledge the financial support of the Government of
Canada through the Canada Book Fund and of the Province of
British Columbia through the Book Publishing Tax Credit.

This book was produced using FSC®-certified,
acid-free papers, processed chlorine free, and printed
with soya-based inks.

Printed in China
27 26 25 24 23   1 2 3 4 5

For Caley

sipster

sip·ster | \ sip-stər \

: one who observes, seeks, and sets taste trends of sipping beverages, such as wine, spirits, tea, and coffee, outside of the mainstream.

CONTENTS

INTRODUCTION 2

SPARKLING WINES 19

WHITE WINES 31

ROSÉ WINES 67

RED WINES 79

DESSERT WINES 117

SIPSTERS' CODE OF CONDUCT 128

SIPSTER'S GUIDE TO PERFECT PAIRINGS 129

GENERAL TOURING INFORMATION 132

CONFESSIONS OF A SIPSTER 135

CHEERS TO WONDERFUL PEOPLE 137

INDEX 138

INTRODUCTION

Welcome to the wonderful world of the sipster! If you take an interest in the things you sip, such as wine, tea, coffee, beer, or spirits, then you may be a sipster yourself.

When I wrote the first Sipster's Guide to British Columbia wine in 2021, I envisioned *sipster* as a more congenial term for someone interested in wine. That level of interest can vary widely, from passionate newbie to someone who holds a certificate or diploma from an accredited wine institution. *Sipster* is a more positive and less condescending descriptor than "wine nerd" or "cork dork." As a merger of *sip* and *hipster*, we can define the term as "one who observes, seeks, and sets taste trends of sipping beverages, such as wine, spirits, tea, and coffee, outside of the mainstream."

The biggest difference between someone who purchases wine regularly and a sipster is the explorative approach they bring to their experience of wine—sipsters enjoy wine on their own terms. They don't need fancy marketing, flowery tasting notes, or random scores to tell them what they can enjoy. A sipster may be completely infatuated with Beaujolais Nouveau at a time when no reviewers would even consider writing about it. A sipster may order a glass of rosé at a steak house because they found one they haven't tasted before, even if it doesn't pair "correctly" with the food they've ordered. Sipsters follow their own palates. Though they appreciate suggestions from wine experts and like-minded friends, they certainly don't rely on either to confirm their enjoyment.

Social media, and the sundry influencers who flock to these platforms, can provide fun tools for exploring new wines, but it can also be detrimental by subtly implying that your own life is inadequate. Influencers and companies try to show you how effortless things could be if you experienced what they experience, the way they experience it. Imagine a simple photo of an influencer with their nose in a glass, looking down to one side, perfectly posed on a ledge overlooking a vineyard. What does that tell you about the wine? Their experience at the vineyard? All this says is "Look at where I am. Don't you wish you were here?"

Sipsters can stick to their guns without feeling the need to go with the crowd. Sipsters don't suffer from fomo—the fear of missing out—but they also don't belittle those who do. Everyone has their own life to live and their own things to experience.

This is the driving force behind the sipster's philosophy: to show that there are many ways to experience wine (or whatever you choose to sip—you do you!). I hope this philosophy also shows wine enthusiasts that the way they experience wine doesn't have to line up with what we've been taught about traditional wine appreciation. Bland descriptors of red berries, hints of wet minerals, and streaks of violets on the back end don't adequately convey the true experience of a wine. If you taste violets on the back end, that's fantastic, but I'm not going to run out and purchase a wine because of it. However, I will seek out a wine that's chatty, happy, or has brought someone to tears because it reminds them of a poignant experience from when they were younger. This is how sipsters enjoy wine. It's all about the *experience*. Strawberries and violets are not experiences in and of themselves.

So, what kind of experiences can we expect to enjoy along with our wine? This has a lot to do with where we are enjoying our beverages and with whom. We can enjoy a wine because of the person we're sharing it with, or because of the weather, or simply because the day leading up to that first sip has been so good. I like to have wine to celebrate occasions no matter how small, but you may pull out a bottle for different reasons, and that's great. Whatever the wine and whatever the occasion, I hope you enjoy that experience to the fullest.

FIRST WINE EXPERIENCES

Most people's first experiences with wine are less than ideal. There are exceptions to this but, in general, our entry wines are inexpensive, monofactured,[1] and bland. Yes, it's possible that, this early in the journey, we don't have enough experience to appreciate *any* wine, but I don't buy that. When something is truly good, it shouldn't be that difficult to suss out. A bad first experience with wine can affect people's attitudes and perceptions about the beverage, and this impression can last for years.

Imagine that you've never eaten a doughnut before. If the first doughnut you ever tried was a bland, mass-produced supermarket variety from a large commercial-industrial bakery, you may well think that this is all the world of doughnuts has to offer. You'd be forgiven for not wanting to try others or explore different flavours. You wouldn't be challenged in your belief that doughnuts aren't worth spending more than a few cents on.

But if your first experience was a freshly made doughnut at a local bakery, your first impression would be very different. That doughnut could have a pillowy texture that melts in your mouth. It could be sweet, but not so sweet as to be cloying and overwhelm the other flavours. Maybe it has nuts or sprinkles for added texture. Or a filling of some kind. Maybe the glaze has a striking cross-hatch pattern that makes it look fantastic. You may start to search out other doughnuts of a similar quality, evaluating them (perhaps subconsciously) and developing personal preferences. You may even seek out artisan bakers or make special trips to visit acclaimed bakeries. Maybe you start sharing your experiences on social media and find others who have enjoyed different styles or flavours.

I don't recall my first experience with wine. My parents only had what I would now call "wine-like beverages" on special occasions or when there were parties. I don't remember any special conversations about wine—it was just another thing for them to drink or offer guests. To be fair, most of the

---

1 Monofacturer: a company that produces one product in versions that differ only slightly.

wines produced in Canada at that time were monofactured imitations of European wine styles.

Later, when I was in university, whisky and Scotch were my primary beverages of interest. It wasn't until later, when I had a girlfriend whose family drank wine regularly at dinner, that I experienced what wine can do when it's paired with a meal—it changed my world forever. Though I don't recall what that first wine was, I do recall my first experience with a Canadian wine. It was a Jackson-Triggs Cabernet Sauvignon. My girlfriend and I were having dinner with another university couple and had asked them to bring wine and a dessert. They showed up with two bottles of the J-T Cab, a 40 ounce of rum, two 2 litre bottles of Coke, and a pie from the supermarket. It was a fantastic evening of food and conversation, insofar as our humble student budgets allowed.

I later learned that the Jackson-Triggs wines that I had enjoyed that night were referred to as entry-level wines.[2] In the industry, "entry-level" refers to the least expensive wines in a winery's portfolio. The idea is that, as the most financially accessible bottles, these wines are the most likely to be purchased first by the widest number of people. Later, satisfied customers may seek out the brand's more expensive wines. Some wineries make tons of entry-level wines as they are less expensive to produce.

When these wines are done right, they can be incredibly good value. But how do you decide which entry-level wines to try? This isn't easy to predict because everyone has different tastes. How do you figure out what *you* like?

EXPERIENCING WINE

When I first got into wine, I did what I normally do when I develop a new interest: I read about it. A lot. I bought books. A lot of books. I searched online. A lot of searching. However, with wine, I found it very difficult to connect what I read to what I experienced when I actually drank it. I learned a lot

2 In one of those full-circle life moments, I got to tell the story of that dinner to Donald Triggs when I interviewed him for my first book.

from reading, but my drinking experience was limited by my budget. With time, I realized that the money I'd spent on reference books could have been better spent on wine instead. If the wine books didn't effectively translate the experience of drinking wine into words, there had to be a better way. The Sipster's series is the direct result of this quest to find a new way to write about wine.

When I started to really experience wine in wine country, many of my tasting experiences were uncomfortable. Just like the books had failed to adequately communicate the wine experience to me, most winery bars did not feel like places where I would normally enjoy wine. It was okay if the wine shop wasn't too busy, but crowded ones were the worst. Standing sideways at a crowded and noisy tasting bar with forty other people vying for the attention of the staff simply wasn't the best way for me to enjoy wine. Until the recent pandemic made wineries realize that there are more profitable ways to showcase their wines, I felt like I was the only one who was irritated by this. More often than not, I enjoy my wine sitting at a table or in a comfy chair. Standing up at a tasting bar is like test driving a new car by cruising around the parking lot. When I test drive a car, I want to take it on the road.

Tasting notes, either from a winery or a reviewer, didn't help either, as they often misplace our real sense of a wine's value. They build up wines using long lists of aromas, flavours, and miscellaneous production facts. Some of this information is useful if you're involved in the wine industry—salespeople, sommeliers, and chefs all need more technical information for food-pairing techniques—but most of this isn't going to help you find a new wine you enjoy. Do people really taste wine like that? What other product sells itself as tasting *like* something else? Try our strawberries—they taste like strawberries. Well, they'd better!

As wine importer Terry Theise once said, "wine is a moving target." Even expert wine judges, who are certainly highly skilled tasters, can come to different conclusions about the same wine. Human chemistry, environmental factors, and preconceived perceptions about a wine (which can be as simple as seeing its colour before tasting it) will alter how much or how little we enjoy a wine. As Bianca Bosker says in her recent book *Cork Dork*, "no taste is pure."

There must be a better way to learn about and experience great wines.

HOW WINES ARE TRADITIONALLY EVALUATED

TASTING NOTES

Communicating about wine is a serious issue, for those in the industry and for those who love to read and write about it. It's all become a bit silly over the past few decades because we haven't developed the language to talk about wine effectively. Communication about any art form has the same problem. As the popular quote goes, "writing about music is like dancing about architecture."[3] How does one distill an art form that needs to be experienced? How can that experience be accurately communicated to other people who have not experienced it and cannot possibly experience it in the same way as the writer?

Traditional wine communication has focused on tasting notes, using snippets of snappy language to list the aromas and flavours the writer perceived when they sampled a wine. This language is everywhere, in newspaper reviews, wine magazines, blogs, and on wine apps. To prepare for a review, the writer will likely taste a wine aggressively, a style that aims "a beam of concentrated attention directly at the wine, using [one's] palate to take a sort of snapshot," according to Terry Theise's *Reading Between the Wines*. Wine students use this technique when studying wine, and it must be learned and practiced regularly to achieve consistency. It's not an easy method, but almost anyone can learn to do it.[4]

Tasting notes are a relatively new concept in the industry, though their ubiquity for today's wine lovers makes them seem

---

3 This quote has been attributed to the comedian Martin Mull and the composer Frank Zappa, among many others.
4 Conditions like anosmia, wherein a person loses the ability to smell, can drastically impair the efficacy of this method. Unfortunately, some in the industry have experienced this recently as a symptom of Covid.

as if they've been around since wine's conception. This would be true if wine had been invented in early 1970s California, but of course it was not. Credit for the vocabulary that added rocket-fuel to tasting notes goes to Ann Noble of the University of California, Davis, who developed the Wine Aroma Wheel. The inner sectors of this brilliantly designed wheel contain general aroma groups: fruity, herbaceous, floral, woody, earthy, or chemical, among others. These groups are then broken down in the following sectors, moving away from the centre of the wheel. *Fruity* breaks down into all the different families of fruit, such as citrus, berry, tree fruit, or tropical fruit. Those categories can break down even further. If it's a berry flavour, what kind of berry? Currant? Blackberry? Strawberry?

The Wine Aroma Wheel outlined a simple system, which allowed us to create a vocabulary for the things we smell—something that English as a language has never really emphasized. Plato deemed our sense of smell unimportant and unbecoming of a civilized, rational person, and following in these footsteps, English has few aromatic descriptors and expressions. For example, take the way we describe cheese. The French language has expressions such as "les pieds de Dieu," which is an elegant way to denote the stinky character of some cheeses. "The feet of God" in French; *stinky* in English. Which version sounds more enticing?

Noble's aroma wheel provided a brilliantly simple solution to a complex problem in a language that lacked the vocabulary to describe our sense of smell. For students studying wine, wine enthusiasts, and anyone related to the industry, it works. But for me, and perhaps for most people, this list of aromas was perplexing at first, particularly when it came to wines from lesser-used regions of the wheel—"Wet wool"? "Diesel"? I should want to drink that? Why is my wine proffering aromas and flavours anyway? What good does that do? Shouldn't all wine just taste like wine? If a wine smells of candied strawberries, tastes like dried herbs, and has a long, dry finish, what am I meant to glean from this information? The obvious answer is that if you like eating or smelling these things, then you have a good chance of enjoying the wine. If a wine has notes of cranberries and you do not like cranberries, then what are the odds that you will like the wine? Probably fairly low. What if the idea of tasting cranberries in a wine is completely weird to you? Average wine consumers don't have a lot of information to go on with tasting notes like this. No wonder people are confused! As Bianca Bosker says in *Cork Dork*, tasting notes "are now badly failing the very people they're meant to help."

Even if you avoid reading about wine, this style of communication is used in other ways, most significantly as part of the wine-shop experience. Visitors are given a small (sometimes pathetically small) sample of wine while the person behind the bar spouts off the list of aromas and flavours they should experience when they smell and taste the wine. One of two things will happen in this scenario: (1) the taster will imagine that they smell and taste all the flavours the host has told them to when, in reality, they don't taste any of those things; or (2) the taster will feel stupid for not tasting those things and assume they just aren't a good enough taster to enjoy the wine. I'm convinced that both of these scenarios factor into how different wines can taste once visitors return home after a trip to wine country. Ever opened a bottle you purchased at a winery or a tasting and thought, *Wow, this doesn't taste anything like I remember from the wine shop*?

If only there were an even simpler way to describe a wine's qualities.

POINT SCORES

Well, there is a simpler way to describe wine quality, but perhaps it's too simple. I'm referring to a wine's rating or score. Older rating systems ranked wines out of 20 or 10, while newer systems sometimes use letter grades or icons such as stars or grape bunches. But the most universally praised system in North America is the 100-point scale, which was created by the wine critic and demigod Robert Parker in the mid-1970s, around the same time Ann Noble was developing the Wine Aroma Wheel. It caught on quickly because it resembled school test scores. If you receive a 95 on a quiz, then you know you did well, much better than your friend who received 76.

But there are problems with using point scores for rating wine. Perhaps at one time they made sense for measuring a students' progress in school, but a bottle of wine isn't measurable in the same way. Is a 90-point wine really that much better than an 88-point wine? What if you like the 88-point wine better?

When I was new to wine, point scores were a helpful and easy way to choose wines. I figured that if someone else thought these were good wines, then I would learn more about what good wine was by drinking them. There was usually an agreement between the scores and the wines I got to taste—the bottles I liked better tended to be scored a little higher than the ones I found less impressive. But the reality was that I wasn't tasting a wide variety of wines because I only bought those with higher scores. Was I learning about what made a wine good for myself? Or was I simply being taught what I *should* like?

Point scores started to mean less to me, particularly when it came to assessing Canadian wines, which seemed to have a definite quality ceiling. In Canadian wine magazines in the early 2000s, most Ontario and British Columbia wines were scored between 85 and 89 points. There were exceptionally few 90- or 91-point wines, and only Icewines were ever given higher ratings. The highest-rated table wines were always from Old World regions, like Bordeaux, or California. I knew there were some amazing wines being produced here, and yet they still received middling scores. I started to question what these scores meant and why I even cared. The same wine could be given drastically different scores by different critics. Which one was more accurate? Who was correct? I also experienced amazing wines that I found out later only received middling scores. Point scores came to mean less and less to me as I shopped for wines. After all, why should we reduce the wine experience to a mere numeral?

To help illustrate the pointlessness of scores, consider scoring other artistic things in our lives like television shows, paintings, or music. "In that last episode of *Schitt's Creek*, David and Alexis weren't really all that funny. I'd give it only 81 points." What does that prove? About as much as giving 90 points to Claude Monet's 1903 painting *Nymphéas*. "It looks like he didn't even paint the entire canvas, so I had to take points away for that." No matter that the water in the painting looks like it's actually shimmering and that the water lilies seem to float in three dimensions as you change your viewing angle; Monet didn't make use of the whole canvas, so therefore he should lose points. Movies get ratings from film critics too, but how often do we pay attention to them? They still kept making Transformers movies, so clearly ratings don't make that much of a difference.

As my career took me into wine sales, the value of point scores became more obvious. They are undeniably useful tools to market and sell wine. They hooked me when I was learning about wine and spurred me to hunt down specific, high-scoring vintages. Points can be a useful shorthand as you begin your journey of learning what makes a good wine. Once we learn what we like, points become less necessary, and we can judge for ourselves more effectively. If you want wines that other people have awarded high scores, then keep following along. Go with the crowd, enjoy your wine, and have a great time. This book takes a very different approach.

THE SOLUTION: WINE EXPERIENCES

If you want to venture out on your own and find the hidden gems of Ontario wine, the ones that don't necessarily win awards or get high scores,[5] this is the book for you! In it, I present a new way of thinking about wine to help *you* decide which wines to pick up on your next trip to the store or wine country. Rather than focusing on the flavours, aromas, and amazing production techniques, I focus on the experiences these wines inspire. Well-made wines have their own styles and personalities. Some wines are serious and philosophical. Others have a more rambunctious attitude. Some are widely appealing crowd-pleasers, while others are accessible only to those who take the time to appreciate nuances. Just like humans, wines can be adventurous, silly, complex, wild.

All of the wines in this book were selected because I believe they are worth experiencing. Some of them I really like, and

5 Both of which a winery has to actively seek out for the sake of their marketing. Some fantastic wineries don't even bother.

some aren't to my personal taste, though I recognize their value as excellent wines. What unites them all is that they are very well crafted. Every wine in Ontario is good for someone. The ones I've chosen to include here are special because their qualities can't be explained simply by tasting notes or point scores. A wine can have a lot to say, or very little. The best experiences come when a chatty wine is paired with an experience in which we are primed to listen to what it has to say.

You can find some truly amazing wines in Ontario that won't set off your banking app alerts. All the wines described in this book retail for under $50 on the winery's website, and most of them are surprisingly priced for the level of quality. Some are a little more difficult to find, while others are widely available. All of them are waiting for you to search them out and share them.

I hope this book will spark your sense of adventure while giving you more confidence in your own palate. Maybe you'll try some new varieties or styles you weren't daring enough to consider before. There's a lot to discover in the world of wine, even within a single wine region. Did you know that there are tons of wineries *outside* the Niagara Peninsula?

After years in the wine industry, I have learned that there are people out there who hate wines I love and love wines I don't enjoy. The reality is that all winemakers work to produce the best wines they can. Any bottle out there can be somebody's favourite. So how are we supposed to choose?

"What's in your glass should never be more important than who you are sharing it with," according to Mike Nierychlo, who co-owns Emandare Vineyard with his wife, Robin, in Duncan, British Columbia. He's been saying this for years, even placing it as a prominent heading on the winery's website. This is one of my favourite quotes about wine because it's a salient reminder that knowing a wine was aged for 17 months in new French oak and has aromas of black currants doesn't mean that it will be the perfect wine for a romantic date night or a full-contact game of Cards Against Humanity. The purpose of wine is to enjoy it with the people who are special to us. If it's a special person, make it a special wine.

A NOTE ON HOW THE WINES WERE TASTED

All of these wines were enjoyed with food, using various styles of wineglasses in real-world wine enjoyment situations. The glasses ranged from high-quality stemware to the thick-rimmed wineglasses my daughter gave me for Christmas, bought years ago at her elementary school's Santa's Workshop sale. I even used stemless wineglasses—*gasp*! Essentially, I used just about any glass designed for drinking wine. No mugs, tumblers, or juice cups were used.

I did follow some wine protocols to give each wine the chance to taste its best. These protocols came from my formal wine training and many years of pouring wine professionally. The wines were served at their proper serving temperature. White wines, rosés, Icewines, and sparkling wines were chilled and reds, with only a few exceptions, were not. All wines were paired with a suitable food and occasion, when possible. I immediately wrote down my notes and experiences with each wine, often with some still in my glass.

HOW THE WINES ARE PRESENTED

WINERY AND WINE NAME

WINERY PRICE: ♥ = < $10
♥ ♥ = $10–20
♥ ♥ ♥ = $20–30
♥ ♥ ♥ ♥ = $30–40
♥ ♥ ♥ ♥ ♥ = $40–50

BODY: LIGHT/MEDIUM/FULL
SWEETNESS: DRY/OFF-DRY/MEDIUM/SWEET/LUSCIOUS
ATTITUDE: THE WINE'S PERSONALITY

Pair with: Foods, moods, and occasions

WINERY PRICE: This is the approximate price range of the wine, pretax, as listed on the winery's website. Prices are subject to change at the whim of the winery, of course, so none of the prices listed here are set in stone. They will give you a general sense of what you can expect to pay.

BODY: When wine people talk about the body of a wine, they are referring to the perceived fullness or texture of the wine. I like to describe this in terms of milk. Skim milk feels light and watery. Move up to 2% milk, and the texture feels a bit fuller. Homogenized milk will be even fuller, and 10% cream even more so. Wine can be the same way—watery and thin or thick and full. It has nothing to do with the intensity of the flavour, only the sensation of the texture.

Why does this matter? It matters because it affects what you pair the wine with—foods or occasions. The weight of the wine needs to match the weight of the food and the occasion. Hosting a reception outside at your wedding in July? A big-bodied red wine probably won't be what you're looking for because, in the hot sun, nobody will want to drink it. It probably won't work with that cedar-planked salmon on the grill either.

SWEETNESS: During my years in wine sales, I found this was usually one of the first three questions customers asked me, along with "What are the grape varieties?" and "How much is it?" It's also one of the most misunderstood factors, so let me try to clear this up. *Dry* means "no sugar" so therefore not sweet at all. *Off-dry* means that there is a little bit of sugar, and to some people, it can taste a little sweet. Most people will probably find it still tastes dry but that it has a smoother mouthfeel. I've actually had a person taste a late-harvest dessert wine—a wine that is *legally mandated* to be sweet—and say, "Oh, that's quite dry."

All I do is nod and silently quote a line from *The Princess Bride*: "You keep using that word. I do not think it means what you think it means."

Winemakers need to be aware of a wine's sweetness because the sugar and acidity need to be balanced. Think of it like lemon juice. If you squeeze a lemon to make lemon juice, what do you need to make it drinkable? Sugar! Sugar is what balances the high acidity of the lemon, and *voila*—a refreshing beverage on a hot summer day. If there isn't enough sugar, it will taste sour. Too much sugar, and it tastes cloying. Getting that balance right is the key.

Ontario wines naturally have more acid compared to those made in hotter wine-growing regions, so a little residual sugar can make them balanced. Right now, it is more acceptable for white wines to have higher levels of residual sugar than reds. Red wines in Ontario are generally fermented completely dry, with no residual sugar at all.

If the vintage is successful and the winemaker has done a good job, most people won't even notice that there is sugar in a wine. It will simply taste well made. Sugar is not bad or good. It's there for balance. We've had a couple of generations of wine lovers who grew up thinking that they were not supposed to like sweet wines. If you are concerned about getting headaches from sweeter wines, consider drinking less in an evening. Problem solved.

ATTITUDE: This is where my wine descriptions really start to diverge from the norm. The characteristics mentioned so far are based on more measurable factors, with body being the description of texture and sweetness being an assessment of sugar, which can be accurately measured through laboratory analysis.

Aroma descriptors are not nearly as measurable, and writers must rely on similes to get their points across. One could say that a wine "smells like" black currants, dried mangoes, or tennis balls, but that doesn't mean that the wine has those aromas deliberately built into it (though if you are new to wine, I can see how easy that is to assume). This is one person's perception of the wine, and we assume that they are adequately qualified to make their assessments. Were they trained as a winemaker, sommelier, or educator? With the Court of Master Sommeliers? The International Sommelier Guild? The Wine & Spirit Education Trust? To what level? Does that even matter?

Training inconsistencies aside, the use of aromatic descriptors alone is a limited way to describe wine, when it can be evoked using other linguistic devices. Aromatic similes can go only so far, but images and metaphors can help us understand a wine more deeply. Opening it up gives us a whole new range of instruments to communicate a wine's personality. Lots of wines have "aromas of strawberries and dried herbs," but only this one can be described as being "like a relaxing breakfast with waffles and fresh berries." Some wines are hidden or coy, while others are bombastic or vivacious. Wines are not just wines; they can be like people. They can have attitudes and personalities. The ultimate wine pairing occurs when the right wine is matched to the right situation.

PAIR WITH: Wines are almost always paired with food, although even this is a relatively recent phenomena in wine consumption. Suggestions for food pairings are common in the marketing material provided by wineries, as well as in the banter spouted by eager wine-shop sales staff. There are many books and college courses dedicated to the concepts surrounding these pairings, and learning these techniques is a great way to increase your enjoyment of wine during meals.

But what if you don't happen to have duck confit and cherry gastrique prepared tonight and just want to enjoy a wine on its own? What if you want to have a glass while watching the sunset? What about the best wine for a relaxing bath, or a late-spring picnic?

Matching wine to food is important, but matching it to the occasion should enhance the enjoyment of both all the more effectively and deeply. At its most basic, a truly great pairing occurs when these things mutually reinforce each other without one overshadowing the other. The wine should make the food taste better, and the food should make the wine taste better. The same goes for the occasion: the wine should help make it that much more memorable.

In this book, I list possibilities for foods, occasions, and moods that I believe will pair beautifully with these wines. You can also use the index at the back and search through the pairing list to find the perfect wine.

Happy sipping!

❑ ANGELS GATE
SPARKLING CHARDONNAY 21

❑ CHÂTEAU DES CHARMES WINERY
ROSÉ SPARKLING 23

❑ KEW VINEYARDS
PINOT MEUNIER SPARKLING 25

❑ MAGNOTTA BLANC DE NOIRS
SPARKLING WINE 27

❑ PELLER ESTATES ICE CUVÉE CLASSIC 29

SPARKLING WINES

So, here we go with the fizz properly at the front! Starting a meal or a special event with a bottle of bubble brings out the smiles in everyone. It's like we, as humans, have learned that the pop of a sparkling wine's cork is the official start of whatever fun is about to happen—"Paging Doctor Pavlov. Please report to the wine cellar."

It is good to celebrate things when we can. I would argue that the pandemic has helped us appreciate the good things we have in life. I would also argue that corralling sparkling wine into the pen allocated only for special occasions means we miss out on many wonderful pairing experiences. Ever had sparkling wine with beef? No? That's a shame. How about with popcorn?

Sparkling wine is in fact wine and can be properly matched with any food or occasion, just like any other category of wine. It doesn't have to be a special occasion, nor does it have to be the only bottle of the night. We are lucky that Ontario wineries have really stepped up to produce some amazing sparkling wines for all occasions. Try a multi-course meal accompanied only by sparkling wines. Or reverse the traditional pairing sequence and pour the sparkling wine last with dessert! Can it be done? Of course!

That's what makes a life of wine so interesting. Cheers to that!

Do hummingbirds feel this way as they hover over their flower-shaped feeders?

ANGELS GATE
SPARKLING CHARDONNAY

WINERY PRICE: 🍷 🍷 🍷
BODY: LIGHT
SWEETNESS: DRY
ATTITUDE: DREAMY

Pair with: Canapés, light desserts, backyard fires

Have you ever had one of those dreams where you're floating on air? You could be high in the sky or close to the ground; all that matters is the weightlessness. Do hummingbirds feel this way as they hover over their flower-shaped feeders? They seem to float in place, oblivious to wind or obstacles in their path.

Perhaps our human desire for weightlessness drove us to invent the airplane. Maybe we equate flight with a particular sense of freedom. Kids delight in this feeling on playgrounds, swinging and sliding and spinning on great metal wheels. If you were that kid in elementary school who tried to leap off the swings at the top of their arc—there's always one[6]—then you know how awesome freedom can be. It's worth the risk of leaping.

This wine tastes like weightlessness, lovingly bottled so that you can put it in the fridge the night before a special dinner. As you sip, you'll experience the carefree, no-strings-attached existence of a hummingbird in the form of wispy aromas and a beautifully cleansed palate. If the dry mustiness of some sparkling wines has kept you from exploring the style in the past, this sparkling Chardonnay will send you floating away on a sea of dreaminess.

---

6 I was one of those kids.

I hope that picnics
don't go the same
way that candles
did for my parents.

CHÂTEAU DES CHARMES WINERY ROSÉ SPARKLING

WINERY PRICE: 🍷🍷🍷🍷
BODY: LIGHT
SWEETNESS: DRY
ATTITUDE: SOCIAL

Pair with: Spinach salad, chicken skewers, picnics

For a lot of people, wax candles are a special treat. We use little ones on birthday cakes to commemorate another trip around the sun and place a pair on the table for a romantic dinner with our sweetheart. For years after the infamous ice storm that hit eastern Ontario and Quebec in 1998, my parents stopped using candles. Special dinners became strictly lights-on occasions. The simple delight of a burning candle was ruined by their experience of one of the country's worst natural disasters. As their main light source during this time, candles lost their romance in favour of utility. You might as well stick little flashlights in birthday cakes as far as they were concerned.

I hope that picnics don't go the same way that candles did for my parents. As one of the only safe, socially distanced ways to gather for casual meals during the height of the pandemic, picnics have suffered from overuse. Where they used to be casual, celebratory gatherings to share food alfresco, picnics became one of the only ways to socialize with friends and loved ones outside of your Covid bubble.

Sparkling rosé may be suffering a similar fate. There are still people who think all pink wines are sweet and, therefore, inferior. Though rosé may have been more utilitarian in one's early drinking years, adults often see it as a silly, youthful style that they have outgrown. Unfortunately, this leaves a lot of amazing wines, including this one, on the shelf. Sipsters know that all wine styles can be fantastic, if done right, and this one is solidly in the "done right" category. If you haven't experienced a beautiful sparkling rosé before, this should be your introduction.

It wouldn't take long to graduate into full-on laughter.

KEW VINEYARDS
PINOT MEUNIER SPARKLING

WINERY PRICE: 🍷 🍷 🍷
BODY: MEDIUM
SWEETNESS: DRY
ATTITUDE: GARDEN PARTY

Pair with: Light cheeses, strawberry desserts, frolicking

The radio station at my university had a wild record collection. In it was a set of records that contained nothing but people laughing. Sometimes it was a male laughing, sometimes a female. Sometimes it was a small group of people, and sometimes it was a large group. I assume these tracks were meant to be used as sound effects for shows and theatre productions.

The silly thing was that whenever one of these tracks played, it only took a few seconds for me to start smiling. That smile would then turn into a chuckle, which would proceed to a giggle and then on to a chortle. It wouldn't take long to graduate into full-on laughter.

I should point out that this university had a strict "no smoking anything" policy, so we couldn't giddy-up that way. Nor was there any alcohol involved, even with the unofficial "Apple Juice Rule" in the dorm hallways (wherein the supervisors assumed that any drink they saw was apple juice, even if it had obvious foam on the surface).

This wine is the laugh track that almost forces you to giggle along with it. One whiff of the beautiful aromas will bring a smile to your face. After taking a sip and feeling the creamy mousse of the bubbles, that smile is all but guaranteed to turn into a chuckle. Once you reach chortle status, be careful when you sip. You won't want to waste one drop of this wine.

If there's sparkling wine, there's something to celebrate.

MAGNOTTA
BLANC DE NOIRS SPARKLING WINE

WINERY PRICE: 🍷🍷🍷
BODY: MEDIUM
SWEETNESS: OFF-DRY
ATTITUDE: INTIMATE

Pair with: Baked Brie, full-flavoured seafood, hot tubs

By their nature, sparkling wines have always been given the task of party planner. No offense to any other beverage manufacturers out there, but when there's a sparkling wine, you've got a real party. Drivers don't pop open large cans of cola and douse each other with it at the end of a Formula 1 race. Everyone would be very sticky if they did, but more importantly, the ritual wouldn't have the same meaning. If there's sparkling wine, there's something to celebrate. Even if there are only two people around to share it. Or *especially* if there are only two people.

This is an intimate wine—I mean private-hot-tub-for-two *intimate*—and that makes it perfectly suited to personal celebrations. An anniversary. A reunion after a long time apart. The commemoration of a cherished achievement. There are many situations where only one other person knows the significance of an occasion. Imagine them holding an empty glass as they wait for you to twist off the muselet (six times, of course) and safely pop the cork. The anticipation builds and you pour the wine into their waiting glass and then your own. Clink, take a sip, and let the evening lead you where it will.

Does it ever
taste GOOD and
COMPLEX and FULL
of amazing flavours.

PELLER ESTATES ICE CUVÉE CLASSIC

WINERY PRICE:
BODY: MEDIUM
SWEETNESS: MEDIUM SWEET
ATTITUDE: JOVIAL

Pair with: Salty cheeses, spicy food, good times

<sip>

Wowthiswineisreallyreallygoodbutit'salsogotsomesugartoit so it's like really really yummy and there are beautiful aromas, like TONS of beautiful aromas of things that I've totally never smelled before because the label said that Ice wine was added to it before it was bottled (that's called the "dosage") and, yes, it does make it a little sweet but that shouldn't keep you away from this wine because, wow, does it ever taste GOOD and COMPLEX and FULL of amazing flavours, some of them are probably because of the Ice wine because there are some frosty notes when I smell it but not when I taste it and I will certainly add this to my shopping any time I need a beautiful sparkling wine that is appealing to lots of people and it will make them happy, even if they aren't really happy before they taste or if they're having an off day of some kind, I mean I have no idea what people are going through on any given day I should probably try to pay more attention to that kind of thing and maybe I'll put that on my list for next New Year's Eve because it would totally go with any desserts that people have at parties like that but it could also go great with spicy food too, like chocolate with chili powder on it, have you ever had that, it's unreal and seems totally weird but it isn't for some reason it tastes totally normal and a total contrast in tastes that, I don't know, just seems to work so try it if you're ever offered that kind of thing.

<sip>

❏   **CAVE SPRING RIESLING**   33

❏   **FLAT ROCK CELLARS
NADJA'S VINEYARD RIESLING**   35

❏   **KIN VINEYARDS CHARDONNAY**   37

❏   **MINDFUL PINOT GRIGIO**   39

❏   **ON SEVEN THE PURSUIT CHARDONNAY**   41

❏   **OXLEY ESTATE WINERY AUXERROIS**   43

❏   **PARADISE GRAPEVINE GOLDEN HOUR**   45

❏   **PENINSULA RIDGE ESTATES WINERY
SAUVIGNON BLANC**   47

❏   **QUEENSTON MILE VINEYARD CHARDONNAY**   49

❏   **REIF ESTATE WINERY RESERVE PINOT GRIGIO**   51

❏   **ROSEWOOD CELLARS LEGACY SPICED MEAD**   53

❏   **SUE-ANN STAFF ESTATE WINERY RIESLING**   55

❏   **TRAIL ESTATE WINERY CHARDONNAY**   57

❏   **TWENTY BEES PINOT GRIGIO**   59

❏   **VINELAND ESTATES WINERY
CHARDONNAY MUSQUÉ**   61

❏   **WAUPOOS ESTATES WINERY AUXERROIS**   63

❏   **WAYNE GRETZKY ESTATES SAUVIGNON BLANC**   65

WHITE WINES

Ontario has been making world-class white wines for a long time, but does anyone notice? The province's Icewine received international attention early on and continues to garner the recognition it deserves. But what about whites? White wines aren't considered as serious as red wines, which are still lauded as more prestigious and valuable. The reason? Reds supposedly age for longer and often cost more.

Bunk. A white wine can live just as long, and often longer, than a red wine. And just because a wine is red, it doesn't mean that it will age well. Some white wine styles can be extraordinarily long lived. A decades-old Ontario Riesling is a magnificent tasting experience, one that changes your perspective on aged wines entirely.

Of course, making a wine that's suitable for aging sometimes means that it tastes austere and unapproachable when it's young. This also means that most people simply won't like it when they taste it in a wine shop. There are tons of more approachable wine styles, ready to go at a moment's notice. These wines are fantastic for enjoying within three years of the vintage, and few would consider holding on to them for longer. This fresh style has been trendy for years.

Sipsters know the trends, but they can also see past them. It's time that Ontario's white wine got the respect it deserves.

Riesling is like the college party animal that gets straight As.

CAVE SPRING RIESLING

WINERY PRICE: 🍷 🍷
BODY: LIGHT
SWEETNESS: OFF-DRY
ATTITUDE: CAMPUS HOUSE PARTY

Pair with: Shrimp tacos, blackened chicken sandwiches, romantic movies

As a grape variety, Riesling is like the college party animal that gets straight As, seemingly without studying. These grapes make exceptionally high grades look effortless.

When you first meet a Riesling, it can put you off. *Why do I want to smell plastic with flowers and this weird minerally aroma?* It can be a bit rude. Maybe even uncouth. Certainly weird and a bit unapproachable. But there is always that question: *How do they do it?* How does someone so crazy get such good grades and come up with such great ideas?

Cave Spring Riesling displays this style of lateral thinking at its best. On the one hand, it's pure Ontario—flowers and minerals wrapped in a beautifully crisp and balanced package. On the other hand, you can tell that it's done a little travelling outside of the country, studying what Rieslings in other places know. This wine learns from its environment and puts all that information and insight together in the glass. Whether you enjoy it is up to you.

Regardless, this wine certainly has a lot of cool stories to tell.

Below the radar is total sipster territory.

FLAT ROCK CELLARS
NADJA'S VINEYARD RIESLING

WINERY PRICE: 🍷 🍷 🍷 🍷
BODY: MEDIUM
SWEETNESS: OFF-DRY
ATTITUDE: BELOW THE RADAR

WHITE

Pair with: Ham, sautéed trout, convincing friends how good Riesling can be

"Oh, what is this? It smells great!"
"It's from Flat Rock Cellars."
"I know that winery! I've had their Pinot Noir."
"This is their Riesling."
"Their Pinot is *so* f*&king good."
"Yes, well, this is their Riesling—"
"Do you have any of their Pinot Noir?"
"Um, somewhere...How do you like this?"
"I love the Pinot Noir!"
"Uh huh..."

Sometimes when a winery is well known for a particular grape variety, that single variety overshadows lesser-known but equally fabulous wines in their portfolio. This Riesling is one of them, flying low on the horizon, while Flat Rock Cellars' Pinot Noir shows up on everyone's radar. If there's one thing sipsters enjoy, it's hidden gems like this! Below the radar is total sipster territory.

Let's not forget that Pinot Noir wasn't the only grape variety mentioned in the movie *Sideways*. Riesling was mentioned too. Positioned at a slightly awkward moment in the story, it was more of punchline than anything else, but at least it was included. While Merlot sales famously took a dive and Pinot Noir sales spiked after the release of *Sideways*, people barely noticed Riesling in the movie at all.

But it was there. It will always be there. Vive Riesling!

Adventures in wine can happen almost anywhere.

KIN VINEYARDS CHARDONNAY

WINERY PRICE: 🍷 🍷 🍷
BODY: LIGHT
SWEETNESS: DRY
ATTITUDE: EPIC

Pair with: Grilled trout, pesto pizza, listening to '80s vinyl

If there's one thing that unites Canadians, it's that we tend to think people in other places have it better than us. Clearly, this other place (bigger town, bigger city, different part of the same city) has it better than the place right in front of you. It's like modesty with a dash of self-deprecating humour that's gone too far. I've noticed this similar attitude in every province I've lived.

Though wine lovers in Ontario might see other French or Italian wine regions as being better for producing wine than Niagara, other regions in Ontario might look on Niagara as having it pretty good compared to what they have in their region. There's a lot of vineyard land in Niagara, and it's a wonderful place for growing wine grapes. That said, there are wineries scattered around Ontario in places that are not Niagara and that produce truly fantastic wines. Customers may compare these wines to those made in Niagara, prejudging them before they've even had a taste, believing that wines not from Niagara, or a familiar VQA region, may elicit hesitation.

Sipsters know that adventures in wine can happen almost anywhere. They feel no fear about trying wines from new regions and will seek out that rare diamond in the rough. That's how under-the-radar and adventurous these wines can be. The Ottawa region is not Niagara, but wine lovers there can be proud knowing that their region can produce amazing wines, like this one.

This wine is the diamond for which you've been searching. Beautiful, rounded, and the perfect wine to bring to a blind tasting. Get ready to stump everyone.

I vividly recall looking at my nearly naked keychain with a sense of relief and freedom.

MINDFUL

Pinot Grigio

FULL FLAVOURED

1g Sugar/Sucre* | 8% Alcohol

PER 3/4 CUP (175 mL) SERVING | PAR PORTION DE 3/4 TASSE (175 mL)

VQA ONTARIO VQA

750 mL

MINDFUL PINOT GRIGIO

WINERY PRICE: 🍷 🍷
BODY: LIGHT
SWEETNESS: DRY
ATTITUDE: LIBERATED

Pair with: Crisp summer salads, prosciutto, the first hour after work before a long weekend

WHITE

There is a particular feeling of liberation when your obligations are met or your responsibilities are lightened. This feeling came over me when I left a job before moving across the country. For a few days, my keychain was reduced to a single key. The keys for my workplace (two), my apartment (one), my mailbox (two) were all turned in. The single, pathetic key remaining was for a padlock that I'd been using to lock some of my things away in a trunk. I vividly recall looking at my nearly naked keychain with a sense of relief and freedom. I was no longer responsible for locking, closing, or securing everything those keys represented.

This liberation can manifest in many ways. I recall feeling a new sense of freedom when I graduated high school. The obligations of my routine were suddenly cleared away in a single sweeping motion, in the snapshot of being presented a graduation certificate. What was I going to do next? I had an idea, but at that point, there was no rush to make a firm decision. There was time to breathe.

This wine is liberation in a bottle. It's time to breathe. You can enjoy a little more without feeling like you're missing the party. At 8%, this has a lower alcohol content than regular wine, so you can enjoy it at your own pace, without feeling like it's carrying you away.

Sorry, what was
I saying?

ON SEVEN THE PURSUIT CHARDONNAY

WINERY PRICE: ♀ ♀ ♀ ♀ ♀
BODY: MEDIUM
SWEETNESS: DRY
ATTITUDE: SPEECHLESS

Pair with: Poached Atlantic salmon, chicken Kiev, impressing your date

Some wines just leave your mind, your senses . . . overwhelmed . . .

Sorry, what was I saying? This wine is . . .

Wow.

I'm speechless . . . . This is amazing.

Top. Drawer. Chardonnay.

Oh—sorry. You're still reading this?

Sipster's Tip: Do not over-chill this wine. The flavours really start to come out as it comes up to proper temperature. Yes, this seems like a little trouble. Yes, you will absolutely notice a difference. Yes, everyone will notice a difference, not just your sipster friends.

Auxerrois is a grape
that doesn't mind
opening its yearbook.

OXLEY ESTATE WINERY AUXERROIS

WINERY PRICE: ♛ ♛ ♛
BODY: MEDIUM
SWEETNESS: DRY
ATTITUDE: REFLECTIVE

Pair with: Chicken Caesar, grilled veggies, walking down memory lane

High school and university yearbooks occupy a special place in people's lives. That special place is usually the closet. Or the basement. In a box sealed with duct tape. Buried under camping gear.

Some people don't like looking back on these years because of all those awkward teenage moments. Maybe that wasn't the best time in our lives, but in most cases, it had something to do with making us who we are today. The hairstyles and clothes may change, but what about the core of the person who developed alongside those photographs?

Auxerrois is a grape that doesn't mind opening its yearbook and reminding itself of where it came from. It's an intriguing grape variety that doesn't hide its past. Even if you've had a few of them before (there aren't many grown in Canada, let alone Ontario) you might notice how they change with the times and places they're grown. This Auxerrois graduated from a vineyard southeast of Harrow, a very short par three from a giant water hazard called Lake Erie. Undoubtedly, this has effected how the grapes developed in the vineyard and had a huge influence on the wine in the bottle.

There are no secrets with Auxerrois. If it was class clown or voted most likely to succeed, it will be obvious. When paired appropriately with the right food or occasion, it can be a wonderful way to relive the good old days and see how far you—and this grape variety—have come.

This is what Riesling was before it grew up and became all "I'm a big, serious white wine."

2021 Golden Hour
Paradise Grapevine

VQA Ontario VQA

PARADISE GRAPEVINE GOLDEN HOUR

WINERY PRICE: 🍷🍷🍷🍷
BODY: MEDIUM
SWEETNESS: DRY
ATTITUDE: INNOCENT

Pair with: Soft cheeses, salads, picnics on the beach

WHITE

It's time to stop and smell the flowers. If you don't have flowers, this wine can take their place. It is an entire bouquet in a glass. A new and beautiful arrangement of aromas will surround you with each sniff, from the gypsophila (AKA baby's breath) surrounding the bouquet to whatever flowers serve as the main event.

Accompanying all these flowery aromas is a certain rolling-in-the-grass, childlike innocence. This is what Riesling was before it grew up and became all "I'm a big, serious white wine" and "I can age for decades," etc. Wine educators look for something called typicity—the typical flavours that tells us whether a wine is really made with a particular grape—and they will find Riesling's typical flavours in this wine. Except those flavours will show up to the party as a teenager dressed in an Aritzia boyfriend hoodie and worn-out Converse low tops.

Of course, just like teenagers, this wine has a slightly volatile appearance that may be off-putting to traditional wine lovers. It means well, even if it doesn't always show it. The cloudy appearance of this wine won't bother sipsters who know to let it settle for a little bit (or even decant it carefully).

Sipster's Tip: Chilling this wine too much will blunt the aromas, so try not to serve it ice-cold.

Back planted firmly
in the grass, I still felt
like I was flying.

PENINSULA RIDGE ESTATES WINERY SAUVIGNON BLANC

WINERY PRICE: 🍷 🍷 🍷
BODY: MEDIUM
SWEETNESS: DRY
ATTITUDE: PHILOSOPHICAL

Pair with: Spinach pizza, seafood alfredo, stargazing

Staring into the abyss can be fun. It's good to understand that the world is bigger than what you can see, that there are no limits to our perceptions. I recall lying on the ground as a child and staring up at the sky, watching the clouds move. It felt like the earth revolved under me, while the clouds remained still. Back planted firmly in the grass, I still felt like I was flying.

This wine tastes limitless. It's broad and deep in a way that is only possible for wines of this quality. When you taste it, you don't just perceive the aromas or sense the liquid in your mouth—you take in a whole world of information that goes beyond what your brain can process. There's almost too much information. If you've never experienced this before, it can be a little strange, even unsettling. *What is that flavour? Is it good?* Yes, it's good. *What about that other one?* It's weird, but after swirling it around in the glass a little, it's really good. Drinking this wine is like staring into an unlimited sky of flavours.

Is it for everyone?
It should be.

QUEENSTON MILE VINEYARD CHARDONNAY

WINERY PRICE: 🍷 🍷 🍷 🍷
BODY: FULL
SWEETNESS: DRY
ATTITUDE: NOSTALGIC

WHITE

Pair with: Cedar plank smoked salmon, corn chowder, remembering the good old days

If you've ever tasted a wine and thought, *They really don't make things like they used to*, then this wine is for you. This oaked Chardonnay is unapologetic. Is it for everyone? It should be. This style pairs beautifully with the right foods.

The word *Chardonnay* is divisive. People either love it or hate it. The people who say that they don't like Chardonnay actually have their own club. It's called the ABC—Anything But Chardonnay—club. While it seems a bit strange, bashing Chardonnay was in fashion for years. The previous generation of wine lovers simply did not feel that Chardonnay was worth supporting.

Clearly, ABCers aren't sipsters, who are inherently open to all grape varieties and wine styles. Of course, they will have personal preferences (everybody does), but they know that if they actively bash a certain style of wine, they are guaranteed to miss out on some amazing taste experiences. No sipster wants that.

If you've been looking for a buttery, velvety Chardonnay and wonder why it's so difficult to find one, this Queenston Chardonnay is for you. If this style isn't your jam, that's fine too, but you'll be missing out.

It needs to
be heralded.

REIF ESTATE WINERY
RESERVE PINOT GRIGIO

WINERY PRICE: 🍷 🍷 🍷
BODY: MEDIUM
SWEETNESS: DRY
ATTITUDE: REGAL

Pair with: Poached salmon, quinoa salad with fish cakes, heralding

This wine should have its own brass fanfare. It needs to be heralded. If a wine could be royal, this would be one. Hang banners around your dining room if you have them and salute whatever flag is appropriate. Just don't forget to raise a glass in praise of the people who made this amazing wine.

If you need to attract a knight or save a damsel, this wine will help you in your quest. Knights and damsels alike will be impressed. The body of this wine is far from common—remember, this is wine royalty—but it is fantastically rich and satisfying, with mouth-filling flavours and textures that will have you pledging your allegiance to it. The colour is a little deeper than other, more common, wines made from this grape variety. This is *very* special.

If proper protocol is your thing, it's probably best to appoint a town crier as well to let everyone know when the bottle is almost empty.

#thisisamazingmead

SPICED MEAD

ROSEWOOD, 2021

ROSEWOOD CELLARS
LEGACY SPICED MEAD

WINERY PRICE: 🍷 🍷 🍷
BODY: MEDIUM
SWEETNESS: DRY
ATTITUDE: EXOTIC

Pair with: Spiced nuts, plum and cardamom crème brûlée, a day in the snow

#Wow #OMG #sniffysniff #totallyunique
#Iswearyouvenevertastedanythinglikethis #guaranteed
#thisisamazingmead
#whatnevertriedmead? #yourloss

If hashtags are essentially categories for our online thoughts, this will open up a whole new set of hashtags that you've probably never experienced before. Mead rivals wine potentially as the world's oldest human-made beverage. The fun thing about mead (or cider or piquette) is that after spending a lot of time smelling, tasting, and enjoying wine, it can act like a palate cleanser for your senses. It's the same reason that perfume sales counters have a little can of coffee beans to smell between samples of Chanel and Gucci.

The only difference is that, instead of heading back to the wine, this mead's complexities and nuances are more than capable of captivating your senses for the rest of the meal. It's an awesome trip for the truly adventurous sipster.

She was so imaginative that other insults began to pale by comparison.

SUE-ANN STAFF ESTATE WINERY RIESLING

WINERY PRICE: 🍷 🍷 🍷
BODY: MEDIUM
SWEETNESS: OFF-DRY
ATTITUDE: ABRUPT

Pair with: Cabbage rolls, pork chops and apples, deep conversations

When I was in Grade 9, a girl who sat behind me in geography class used to insult me. At first, she was a little annoying, and I tried to steer clear. But she was creative with her insults.

I couldn't help but laugh because they were so funny. After a while, I started to ask her to insult me just to see how creative she could be. Other classmates started to laugh too, and it became the high point of my day. She was so imaginative that other insults began to pale by comparison.[7]

This Riesling reminds me a lot of that girl from Grade 9. It may set you off at first; indeed, the first sip may make you pucker a little more than you were expecting. You might even dread the thought of a second or third sip. But over time, you will start to appreciate that there is a genuine beauty to this wine that makes it brilliant within the context of a great meal. Through the opaqueness of the aromas, there is an incredible intellect, an artistry, and a timelessness of flavour that makes this wine appealing to anyone who enjoys having their senses challenged. If you think that you know all there is to know about Rieslings, this wine will challenge you. And it will keep challenging you as the wine ages and develops a more complex vocabulary—a wonderful experience.

That girl from Grade 9 has remained a close friend. She still sends me insults if I ask, but they are a lot more complex than they were in Grade 9.

---

7 Keep in mind, creative insults have always been an interest of mine. One of my favourite books as a kid was *500 Insults for All Occasions*. So, there's that.

But sometimes being just a little different makes you stand out in a good way.

TRAIL ESTATE WINERY CHARDONNAY

WINERY PRICE: 🍷 🍷 🍷 🍷
BODY: MEDIUM
SWEETNESS: DRY
ATTITUDE: DIRTY DANCING

Pair with: Clam chowder, savoury pizzas, puzzles

WHITE

When something seems like it should be one way but turns out to be totally different, it can be disconcerting. Remember Crystal Pepsi? The clear cola that didn't look anything like it tasted? It was just too different, too weird. Nobody liked it.

But sometimes being just a little different makes you stand out in a good way. Maybe even a great way. This is one of those wines.

This is the most interesting Chardonnay that I've tried in years. It has a unique edge that makes it stand out. The acidity perks you up and makes your food taste more fantastic than it deserves. Only a truly special wine can do that. And yes, there are beautiful flavours and aromas, and, yes, it has a very smooth texture, but what really makes this wine pop is that it has a little spritz. Little bubbles may form around the rim of your glass, heralding one of this wine's unique qualities. This wine is on another level.

As proof, I offer you this: in a tasting that featured eight other bottles of wine, this was the first one to be empty.

They ask the right things about where you're from or where you went to school and then—*bam!*

TWENTY BEES

VQA ONTARIO VQA
PRODUCE OF / PRODUIT DU CANADA
12.5% alc./vol. 750 ml

PINOT GRIGIO

TWENTY BEES PINOT GRIGIO

WINERY PRICE: 🍷 🍷
BODY: LIGHT
SWEETNESS: DRY
ATTITUDE: FRIENDLY

Pair with: Power salads, crab cakes, reconnecting with friends

Some people can talk to anyone in a crowd and make the connection that a perfect stranger has a mutual friend or acquaintance. If they're really good, they can achieve this with only a question or two. They ask the right things about where you're from or where you went to school and then—*bam!*—"Oh, you must know Bob from Halifax." You do know Bob from Halifax, that *specific* Bob from Halifax, and the shock on your face is priceless.

This wine knows Bob. And Jean. And Rhonda. It knows places and people you know. Somehow, this wine connects everyone—in fact, it's a top performer in forging connections. Reconnecting has also become an important occasion of late. As people start travelling again and seeing old friends and family members for the first time in years, this wine can stand back, never dominating the conversation, and foster that feeling of connection.

Just what you need for your next visit.

The outcome could be very exciting.

VINELAND ESTATES WINERY
CHARDONNAY MUSQUÉ

WINERY PRICE: 🍷 🍷
BODY: LIGHT
SWEETNESS: DRY
ATTITUDE: ANTICIPATORY

Pair with: Deep-fried clams, chicken Milanese, enjoying the sunshine

Getting ready for something special can bring butterflies to your tummy—a little jolt of anxiety that provides a burst of energy. The outcome could be very exciting. Maybe you're preparing for a first date, an interview, or a special evening out.

This wine tastes like a boost of psychic energy that builds anticipation for whatever comes next. Getting ready for dinner? Expecting guests any minute? Going on stage in a play? This is your wine.

And don't be put off by that scary word on the label—*Chardonnay*. Don't let that keep you from giving this wine a swirl. It's not the Chardonnay you've tried before. It's more aromatic. It hasn't spent any time in oak. None of those divisive flavours are present. It's a bundle of aromas packaged in refreshing liquid goodness.

Anticipate away—another glass will surely follow.

Take your time.
Your destination will
still be there when
you reach it.

WAUPOOS ESTATES WINERY AUXERROIS

WINERY PRICE: 🍷 🍷 🍷
BODY: LIGHT
SWEETNESS: DRY
ATTITUDE: VACATION

Pair with: Veggies and dip, Cressy pickerel and chips, Frank Sinatra

Vacations do wonderful things to people. Closer to home, they may not be quite as courteous to pedestrians while driving, but on vacation, they are more than willing to wave across a couple of people aiming for the pizza place across the street. The lack of commuting pressure, the absence of a fixed schedule, and the amiability exhibited by locals can inspire the vacationer to slow the heck down and chill. The beach will still be there if you arrive five minutes late.

If any wine tastes like a vacation (and, more specifically, one in Prince Edward County), it's this one. There are no dominating aromas or flavours to push you in one direction or another. Nothing in this wine screams "stay on schedule" or "arrive on time." You're free to wake up with the sun over the water in Waupoos. Sleep in under the covers at your B&B in Wellington. Breathe in the morning air on a morning walk in Hillier. Take your time. Your destination will still be there when you reach it.

The complex simplicity of this wine makes it unhurried. There are flavours and aromas present, if you want them. If you don't, just enjoy the ride. Auxerrois is a largely unknown and underrated but hugely versatile grape variety that, like a yet-to-be-found vacation destination, is waiting to be discovered.

If only we could
simplify our lives
a little.

WAYNE GRETZKY ESTATES
SAUVIGNON BLANC

WINERY PRICE: 🍷 🍷
BODY: LIGHT
SWEETNESS: DRY
ATTITUDE: ACCEPTING

Pair with: Crackers and cheese, salads, lunch with friends

When things get too complex to understand, we have a tendency to ignore them, or worse, disparage them in some way. How many times have you heard someone on the news talking about "the economy" seemingly without understanding a word they're saying or how it relates to daily life? Perhaps we start to tune these things out because we think they don't apply to us. That's just someone yammering away, making something more complicated than it needs to be.

Listening to government officials, public service announcers, or the CEOs of large companies talk about issues, local or national, has a way of making people tune out and resent the things they do hear. I think everyone has been guilty of this at least once: resisting the people who complicate life too much, as if they're somehow trying to make us feel stupid. What do they know, anyway?

Our world is very complicated. Information comes at us from every direction, popping up unexpectedly on the phones and screens we spend so much time on. If only we could simplify our lives a little and just take a moment to appreciate uncomplicated, accessible joy.

That's where this wine comes in. It has happy, welcoming aromas that jump out of the glass, eliciting a joy that far exceeds the wine's price, while the flavours maintain the accessibility that makes you really appreciate the simple things in life.

❏ MINDFUL ROSÉ 69

❏ OXLEY ESTATE WINERY CAB SYRAH ROSÉ 71

❏ PARADISE GRAPEVINE VIN DE SOIF
GAMAY & ZWEIGELT 73

❏ REVEL CIDER IBI APOLLO ROSÉ 75

❏ SOUTHBROOK TRIOMPHE
CABERNET FRANC ROSÉ 77

ROSÉ WINES

Ah, rosé. The wine style that people either love or don't know about. Sipsters love a good rosé because it's food friendly and refreshing to drink even on a humid Toronto summer day. If you're hesitant, just remember that there are beautiful flavours and complex aromas just waiting to be discovered in this underrated wine style.

Rosé is a true friends-with-benefits wine. You can enjoy full flavours without the added commitment of having to eat a particular style of cuisine. Buying Cabernet Sauvignon means that you're committed to having something with big flavours. Pouring a light Pinot Gris means that steak is out of the question. But rosé will remain by your side, along for whatever culinary ride you choose, often with lower alcohol levels that mean you won't be reminded of your consumption the next morning. It's also great when flying solo. Win-win!

If you haven't tried a rosé in a long time because you think they are all sweet, then please read this section with special attention. Sipsters are often drawn to these beautifully creative, food-friendly, and complex wines.

Need to swim it off in the pool or lake after a great afternoon in the sun?

MINDFUL ROSÉ

WINERY PRICE: 🍷 🍷
BODY: LIGHT
SWEETNESS: DRY
ATTITUDE: ACTIVE

Pair with: Fried chicken, snacks, busy afternoons

Relaxing and taking pleasure in the simple things is a significant part of the wine lifestyle. There are times when enjoying a glass of wine with friends is the best part of our day, our week, or even our year. Sometimes, we just need to be reminded that life needs its slower moments, so we can appreciate the things around us.

This wine is not for those times.

Sometimes you need to *go go go*. This wine won't slow you down. Just gone for a hike up a mountain? This wine will be refreshing without causing your legs to wobble on the way down. Need to swim it off in the pool or lake after a great afternoon in the sun? This wine will let you do just that.

Mindful's rosé will keep you going, offering you a broader view without interrupting whatever pace you want to maintain. As people become more conscious of alcohol's effects, it's good to know that there are satisfying options at lower percentages. Sacrificing flavour is not something that sipsters readily accept, so it's also good to know that these options taste *great*.

ROSÉ

After living slowly for a few years, it feels like many of us are itching to move again.

OXLEY ESTATE WINERY CAB SYRAH ROSÉ

WINERY PRICE: 🍷 🍷
BODY: MEDIUM
SWEETNESS: OFF-DRY
ATTITUDE: FORTISSIMO

Pair with: Grilled pork tenderloin, roast turkey, watching Formula 1

Some people really love going fast. It can be exhilarating to watch things whizz by. But when it comes to speed, perspective is everything. Riding a skateboard close to the ground can make you feel like you're screaming by at a record-setting pace even when, in reality, you're travelling at the geriatric pace of a car in a school zone. Looking out an airplane window, the world appears to slide by slowly, even when you know you're moving remarkably fast. Perspective. It shapes our sense of speed.

Are we craving speed more often these days? After living slowly for a few years, it feels like many of us are itching to move again. Troves of people are lining up at airports, ready to kick-start their reintroduction to the world with travel. Motorcycle sales have been climbing too.

This wine is a foot-down-on-the-pedal, full-throttle, damn-the-speed-limit rosé if there ever was one. In the world of rosé, this is a true rarity. Articulate, pale-coloured, herbal rosés have been the trend in pink wines for the past few years, but this wine is the exact opposite. And it's gorgeous.

My perspective on this wine? I'll have another glass, thank you.

ROSÉ

Here is a hero
to liberate you
from the tyranny
of food pairings.

Paradise Grapevine

2021 Vin de Soif
Gamay & Zweigelt
VQA Ontario VQA

PARADISE GRAPEVINE
VIN DE SOIF GAMAY & ZWEIGELT

WINERY PRICE: ♟ ♟ ♟ ♟
BODY: MEDIUM
SWEETNESS: DRY
ATTITUDE: FREE

Pair with: Your wine glass, that's it, no really

Traditional wine culture often assumes that anyone who drinks wine also wants food pairings to go with it. Wine goes extremely well with food. I've taught college courses dedicated to pairing techniques. When it's done right, a well curated combination can be an unbelievable tasting experience.

Wineries in the classic wine regions of the world—think France, Italy, or Spain, among others—usually pair their wines with established local cuisine. Muscadet and seafood. Provençal rosé with Niçoise salad. Wine regions that don't have decades or centuries of food and wine tradition to fall back on need to get creative to generate pairing possibilities.

New wineries (and wine critics) label wines as "food friendly" to denote that a wine *needs* food to be enjoyed. In reality, the wine itself doesn't need food. It's you, the wine drinker, who needs food to enhance, or blunt, the wine's flavour. It's a subtle way of saying, "This wine isn't good enough on its own, so have this beef tartar as well . . ."

Thankfully, here is a hero to liberate you from the tyranny of food pairings. Vin de Soif (literally "wine of thirst") is the freedom you've been seeking. Beautiful flavours, wonderful textures, and all free of the guilt that comes from the possibility of pairing it incorrectly with your favourite apple, snack, or main course. This is a friends-with-benefits wine, a no-commitment beverage you can swipe right on, guilt free. With around 11% alcohol, it also means that you can enjoy more of it without accidentally dunking your glass into the BBQ.

ROSÉ

You can discuss
it or not.

REVEL CIDER IBI APOLLO ROSÉ

WINERY PRICE: 🍷 🍷 🍷
BODY: LIGHT
SWEETNESS: DRY
ATTITUDE: QUENCHING

Pair with: Fajitas, chicken pizza, swiping right

Anyone who has spent any time on dating apps knows that there are some recurring themes, particularly when it comes to the photos. For every man holding a fish (presumably the manliest activity because, supposedly, they just caught it), there's a woman with a "car selfie" (presumably the absolute best place to take a photo). Add in the obligatory bathing suit shots for both genders, and a feeling of predictability creeps into the whole experience.

For years, wine lovers have considered rosé with this same cynical attitude—*Aren't all rosés sweet? Men don't drink rosé. Rosé? No thanks, I don't need any more candle holders.*[8] This cynicism isn't necessarily without merit. Some of us have had legitimately bad experiences with rosés in the past.

This wine bucks all these trends. Traditional label? No, thanks. Take a look at the lovely art on this wraparound label. Super-sweet? Not at all; this wine is dry. Boring, simple flavours? Never! The wild yeast fermentation makes this a complex wine on the nose and the palate.

It's not easy for a wine to be challenging and yet simple enough to go down easy. You can discuss it or not. Either way, your experience with this wine is going to be a good one.

ROSÉ

8 You might have to ask your grandparents about this reference.

Life is settled,
relaxed, and
wonderfully in
the moment.

ORGANIC
BIOLOGIQUE

SOUTHBROOK

triomphe

CABERNET FRANC ROSÉ
VQA NIAGARA PENINSULA VQA

SOUTHBROOK TRIOMPHE CABERNET FRANC ROSÉ

WINERY PRICE: 🍷 🍷 🍷
BODY: LIGHT
SWEETNESS: DRY
ATTITUDE: INTROVERTED

Pair with: Chilling with snacks, resting without snacks, recovering from a work week

This wine is a holiday where nothing goes wrong and everything exceeds your expectations. If it's a gift-giving holiday, then you get everything you hoped to receive. You see all the people you want to spend time with, and every event you attend is fun and completely drama-free.

Does this seem like a crazy, parallel-universe scenario? Perhaps. But that's what makes this rosé such a thrill to taste. It has everything you want in a rosé and nothing you don't. People who claim not to like sweet rosés will like this one—it's beautifully textured. People who enjoy sweeter rosés will love it for the same magical reason. People who prefer dry rosés will admire it for the beautifully pure flavours. This wine is well balanced, light, and as refreshing as sitting back in your favourite chair, looking at your holiday plans and knowing that everything is exactly where it should be. Life is settled, relaxed, and wonderfully in the moment.

There's nothing left to do but enjoy it.

❏	16 MILE CELLAR REBEL PINOT NOIR GAMAY	81
❏	CLOSSON CHASE CHURCHSIDE PINOT NOIR	83
❏	CLOUDSLEY CELLARS PINOT NOIR	85
❏	DOMAINE QUEYLUS RÉSERVE DU DOMAINE PINOT NOIR	87
❏	EASTDELL CABERNET FRANC	89
❏	FEATHERSTONE CABERNET FRANC	91
❏	FLAT ROCK CELLARS GRAVITY PINOT NOIR	93
❏	HENRY OF PELHAM BACO NOIR	95
❏	LOLA CABERNET SAUVIGNON/ CABERNET FRANC	97
❏	MALIVOIRE FARMSTEAD GAMAY	99
❏	PELLER ESTATES PRIVATE RESERVE CABERNET SAUVIGNON	101
❏	PENINSULA RIDGE ESTATES WINERY RESERVE MERITAGE	103
❏	QUEENSTON MILE VINEYARD PINOT NOIR	105
❏	RENNIE ESTATE WINERY OBSIDIAN CABERNET SAUVIGNON	107
❏	ROSEHALL RUN CHERRYWOOD PINOT NOIR	109
❏	ROSEWOOD "NIGHT MOVES" GAMAY	111
❏	SOUTHBROOK GAMAY	113
❏	TRIUS ESTATES RED THE ICON	115

RED WINES

Red wines made in Ontario have an identity problem. A casual wine drinker, more familiar with inexpensive imported wine, might find Ontario reds lackluster compared to the wines they're used to from California or Argentina. More advanced wine drinkers, some of whom may consider themselves world-savvy consumers, scoff at the reds here. "Pshaw," they say. "That Pinot Noir doesn't taste like a real Burgundy."

No shit. Ontario isn't California, or Argentina, or Burgundy. It's *Ontario*. Canadians can be bashful about their accomplishments, but making assumptions about the quality of Ontario reds that you haven't experienced in a decade seems unfair. Let's appreciate Ontario wines for what they are. Would you stand next to a beautiful waterfall on a Caribbean island and scoff at it because it's not as tall as Niagara Falls? Only Niagara Falls can be Niagara Falls.

Sipsters know that Ontario reds are reaching new levels of quality and coming to unique styles that previous generations of wine lovers may never have experienced. Enjoy these reds for what they are and prepare to be amazed.

Every time you look
at a great piece of art,
there are new things
to discover.

rebel
2018
pinot noir
gamay

GOLD

vqa niagara escarpment vqa

16 MILE CELLAR REBEL PINOT NOIR GAMAY

WINERY PRICE: 🍷🍷🍷
BODY: MEDIUM
SWEETNESS: DRY
ATTITUDE: ARTISTIC

Pair with: Coq au vin, pork tenderloin with mushroom sauce, listening to music without doing anything else

When you're confronted with great art, it can take a long time to perceive everything that a piece has to offer. You can stare at a great painting for hours before you begin to suspect that you've seen all the details. But when you return to the painting after looking at other masterpieces for a while, you'll find even more nuances. Every time you look at a great piece of art, there are new things to discover.

Great music is the same way. There are some songs that you have to hear ten times before you begin to appreciate the artistry. It may take another five listens before you start to think that you understand the song's deeper meanings. Even after that, you begin to hear new instruments and audio affects that you hadn't noticed before. Every time you listen, you catch new phrases, sounds, and melodies. There are a few rare favourites in my album collection that I've been listening to for years, and I still hear new things every time they play.

This wine is great music. It's the song you want to hear over and over again. Every time you put your nose to the glass, it reveals a different scent, a new melody, a hook you hadn't noticed when you took your first sip. Perhaps that first sip felt a bit rough, but less so on the second and third. How does this wine do that?

By the third sniff, you're ready to clean the leaves and pine needles from the eavestroughs.

CLOSSON CHASE
CHURCHSIDE PINOT NOIR

WINERY PRICE: ♈ ♈ ♈ ♈ ♈
BODY: MEDIUM
SWEETNESS: DRY
ATTITUDE: COTTAGE COUNTRY

Pair with: Truffle Brie, tapenades, old rocking chairs

If you have a cottage, you know the particular excitement that comes from making that last turn down the road, right before your beloved home-away-from-home comes into view. All the anticipation—of relaxation, adventure, reprieve from the everydayness of life—is bottled up in that one moment, ready to release on arrival with the first pop of the cork.

This wine is a vacation at the cottage. Consider the aromas. One sniff, and your muscles relax. You're primed for a slower pace. You welcome unpredictability into your daily routine. Another sniff, and you begin a list of everything you need to get the cottage open and ready. By the third sniff, you're ready to clean the leaves and pine needles from the eavestroughs.

Your journey to unwind continues with your first sips. The remarkable complexity of aromas and nuances of flavours in this wine act as catalysts. Not only will you leave your problems behind, but, for the time you are there, you may even forget they exist.

Just like cottage life, every experience with this wine is unplanned and unpredictable. Every visit to the glass yields a new attitude, every sip a new memory. These are the hallmarks of a relaxing cottage experience and a truly great bottle of wine.

RED

Lake Ontario looks like an ocean until you reach the top of the escarpment.

CLOUDSLEY CELLARS PINOT NOIR

WINERY PRICE: ▼ ▼ ▼ ▼
BODY: LIGHT
SWEETNESS: DRY
ATTITUDE: EXPLORATORY

Pair with: Spinach salad, light cheeses, completing a long road trip

Long car journeys are a singular experience. Your body remains in the same place, but you're still moving. The scenery changes. Your point of view changes. The little hill on the horizon as you head north out of Sault Ste. Marie slowly becomes a cliff and then disappears altogether. Lake Ontario looks like an ocean until you reach the top of the escarpment and see the city skyline on the other side. Long flights are similar, but road trips bring you closer to the scenery. You're continually on the brink of seeing something new.

This wine changes in the same way. There are a ton of aromas and flavours that you'll perceive differently depending on how long it's been swirling in your glass. The aromas you smell when you first pour this wine will not last forever. They'll disappear after a few minutes and be replaced by new ones. Like the memories of when you first set out on your journey, the traces of these original aromas will remain in your memory like olfactory palimpsests. Each flavour is a new experience, written over your earliest memories of the journey, that first scent as the wine poured into your glass.

Once you arrive at your destination, you'll realize that even this is only part of the journey.

RED

Your brain will
know it has lost the
argument and accept
defeat with grace.

DOMAINE QUEYLUS RÉSERVE DU DOMAINE PINOT NOIR

WINERY PRICE: 🍷 🍷 🍷 🍷
BODY: MEDIUM
SWEETNESS: DRY
ATTITUDE: ARGUMENTATIVE

Pair with: Soft cheeses, charcuterie, debates

Conversations are conduits for education and communication. Often, saying things out loud crystallizes thoughts and ideas that you didn't even know were possible. The Wright brothers reportedly used this method to troubleshoot the designs of their first airplanes. One brother would take a position and argue it, while the other defended the opposite perspective in a vociferous debate that made the neighbours concerned about all the shouting. At some point, the brothers would swap positions and argue all over again. This may have been concerning for bystanders, but it broadened the brothers' thinking by forcing them to consider often unanticipated problems.

This wine will argue with you in a similar fashion. And it's an amazing experience. Suddenly, flavour combinations that you never thought were possible are bantering back and forth, trying to work out a solution. You brain tries to follow the argument but loses the subtleties as the pace quickens and the intensity increases. Once the dust clears, these flavours are left to linger, and the resulting confluence of ideas becomes amazingly appealing. You might not understand the argument, but damn, this is a bloody fantastic wine.

Arguments like this are often cloaked in wine-speak—obscure tasting notes, point scores, and marketing mumbo-jumbo about terroir-this and vinification-that. No wonder people tune out when wine salespeople ramble on and on. All you need to know is that this wine is fantastic. Your brain will know it has lost the argument and accept defeat with grace.

Time to take another sip.

RED

They take hits from all genres and squeeze them into the zoot suit of a swinging jazz band.

EASTDELL CABERNET FRANC

WINERY PRICE: ♥ ♥ ♥
BODY: MEDIUM
SWEETNESS: DRY
ATTITUDE: SMOOTH JAZZ

Pair with: Roasted pork tenderloin, wood oven pizzas, any band with Bob James playing keyboard

---

For years, smooth jazz was derided for being cheesy. Gen-Xers, who thrashed through their teenage years with '80s arena rock and then grunge music, tended to consider the Paul Anka–style of soft, swingy big-band music a bit old-fashioned. However publicly underappreciated that style was at the time, it's entirely likely that a Diana Krall or Nora Jones album lurked deep in the depths of many a Gen-Xer's CD collection.

Thanks to those Harry Potter–reading, oops-I-did-it-again Millennials, smooth jazz has come back into the mainstream. The excellent musical chops of the early YouTube sensation Postmodern Jukebox is probably behind this, as they take hits from all genres and squeeze them into the zoot suit of a swinging jazz band with wonderful musicianship and high style.

This wine does the same thing with Cabernet Franc. There are none of the rough tannic edges of a hot-climate California Cab, nor are there the grungy aromas of a Chinon. It is just the pure melodies and smooth rhythms of a grape that grows so beautifully in Niagara. The musicianship here is the expert winemaking, keeping the flavour of that melody going without resorting to any special effects or studio trickery.

Pure flavour, smooth as jazz.

RED

Four years may
have passed since
then, or twenty-eight.

FEATHERSTONE CABERNET FRANC

WINERY PRICE: 🍷 🍷 🍷
BODY: MEDIUM
SWEETNESS: DRY
ATTITUDE: PERFECTION

Pair with: Grilled striploin, mushrooms and herbs, reunions

Meeting someone that you haven't seen for years can be daunting. There's no way to predict how it will go. Maybe you're getting together with someone you haven't seen since you were a teenager. Four years may have passed since then, or twenty-eight. No matter the amount of time, the recognition remains the same.

Time has a weird way of connecting the dots. When you finally reunite with this old acquaintance, you discover that they lived in the city for a while. You lived in the same city at the same time and spent unknown hours in close proximity, without ever meeting. How did that happen without either of you realizing? This makes the reconnection feel even more perfect, like it's the destined confluence of your journeys auspiciously timed for this particular moment.

The colours, aromas, flavours, and textures in this Cabernet Franc evoke this through a fantastic wine experience. Each element has taken a separate journey to meet in this special bottle, and pouring it into the glass is a true reunion, experienced as soon as you put your nose in the glass and take that fateful sip.

RED

The bow tie of your meal, the updo of your main course.

FLAT ROCK CELLARS
GRAVITY PINOT NOIR

WINERY PRICE: 🍷 🍷 🍷 🍷 🍷
BODY: MEDIUM
SWEETNESS: DRY
ATTITUDE: FORMAL

Pair with: Duck breast, mushroom risotto, wedding receptions

Some wines are casual. They taste the way dressing in jeans and a T-shirt, or shorts and flip-flops, feels—relaxed and carefree. These wines don't see a need for anything formal.

This is not a casual wine. Sipsters like to have wines for any occasion, but for a lot of people, wine is reserved for formal occasions. There was never wine on my family's table when I was growing up unless there was a special reason—Christmas, New Year's, Easter, or a special dinner with a visiting friend or family member. The presence of wine was what marked these occasions as special, even formal.

This wine is the bow tie of your meal, the updo of your main course. It's that extra-special touch that makes an occasion all the more special. It's the confidence and anticipation that you get after you've dressed in your best formal attire, just before you open the door to leave for an evening out. Are you going to a Christmas party? A special reception? A wedding? Wherever you're going, you're looking and feeling fantastic.

That's how this wine tastes.

RED

This wine is a
little like that
rabbit skewer.

HENRY OF PELHAM BACO NOIR

WINERY PRICE: 🍷 🍷
BODY: MEDIUM
SWEETNESS: DRY
ATTITUDE: UNORTHODOX

Pair with: Gourmet burgers, warmed olives, blind tastings

As a musician I once played at a reception for the owners of a very upscale vacation resort. The chef was known for his creativity, using unorthodox ingredients in relatively traditional ways, and I'd tasted some of his creations before. The food was always delicious and a little different in ways that weren't easy to pin down.

Toward the end of the event, when things had slowed down a little and he had enough time to say hello to everyone, I complimented the food and in particular the chicken skewer that I'd just tasted.

"That's not chicken," he said with a slight smirk.

"Oh! It's fantastic. What is it?"

"It's rabbit."

This wine is a little like that rabbit skewer. When you take your first sip, you may be tempted to call it a Merlot. It's approachable and solid with beautifully dark fruit flavours. But it's different somehow. *Maybe it's a blend of Syrah and Cabernet Sauvignon*, you think, considering its plummy flavours and tannins. But again, it's just not quite the same.

That's what makes this wine really interesting, like the amazing pulled pork slider I had to finish off at that wonderful reception.

"Yeah, that's not pulled pork."

RED

You could always click the "Forgot your password?" link, but that would mean admitting defeat.

LOLA CABERNET SAUVIGNON / CABERNET FRANC

WINERY PRICE: 🍷 🍷
BODY: MEDIUM
SWEETNESS: DRY
ATTITUDE: ACCESSIBLE

Pair with: Chicken or turkey sausages, pasta with pesto, digital detoxes

Everyone uses at least one website that requires an email and password. It may be a store's site that you purchase from once every couple of years, or the site through which you access your child's report cards. For whatever reason, you can never remember that password. You curse the computer upgrade that wiped your log-in credentials.

Of course, you could always click the "Forgot your password?" link, but that would mean admitting defeat. Not an option. You know it, or you did at one point, and you guess again. And again. You pause to jog your memory, consult your little book of passwords to no avail. You're on your own.

This wine doesn't need you to remember your password. No authenticator apps required. It's accessible and ready for whatever meal or occasion you choose to pair it with. The beautiful Cabernet-family flavours are present but without the usual bombardment of tannins that can arise when this variety is grown in hotter climates. Where some Cab Sauvignons yield massive wines with tannins that last for weeks, this one takes a gentler approach. It's not going to dry your mouth out between bites. The texture is smooth, and the flavours are appealing and easy to enjoy.

This is truly accessible flavour at an accessible price.

RED

This may
be humanity's
oldest ritual.

MALIVOIRE FARMSTEAD GAMAY

WINERY PRICE: 🍷 🍷 🍷
BODY: LIGHT
SWEETNESS: DRY
ATTITUDE: SINGALONG

Pair with: Burgers, pasta salads, kumbaya

A certain nostalgia permeates the experience of sitting around a campfire. A backyard fire may unearth memories of Scout camps while a beachside fire with college buddies may inspire memories of family gatherings—the smell of the smoke, the glow of the flames, and the warmth of the coals. Sometimes there are snacks, like s'mores, meant only for fireside enjoyment. Sure, you can make them on a barbeque, but that would be like trying to mass-produce a feeling, one that can only come from sitting next to friends and family around an open fire, trading stories and enjoying the warmth.

At some point, when the light has faded and the gathered people are illuminated only by the flickering flames, someone will start to sing. When everyone knows the words, the sound of unified voices creates an intimate moment where the world stops—everything is here, around this fire. This may be humanity's oldest ritual.

This wine has a warmth, glow, and balance that is perfectly aligned with that inclusive, singalong feeling. Come together now around the fire, sip this wine, and enjoy the ritual.

RED

Your skates glide
over the surface
without any vibration
under your feet.

PELLER ESTATES PRIVATE RESERVE CABERNET SAUVIGNON

WINERY PRICE: 🍷 🍷 🍷
BODY: FULL
SWEETNESS: DRY
ATTITUDE: UNOBTRUSIVE

Pair with: Striploin, lamb stew, snow storms

If you've never skated on a lake in winter, no amount of words in any combination, written or typed out on a page, will ever adequately translate the sensations that come from this truly singular experience. If you have not had the pleasure, you may think, *Oh, it can't be* that *different. It's just ice. All ice is the same.* Wrong. These thoughts immediately betray the fact that you've never taken strides on hard lake ice.

Rare circumstances make skating over a lake possible. You need a combination of very low temperatures and little to no wind to turn a lake into a thick sheet of unending glass. The sensation of gliding over this particular ice is unlike anything else, regardless of how amazing the rink can be. Your skates glide over the surface without any vibration under your feet. This might be disconcerting at first because, when you skate in a rink, there are always textures embedded in the softer ice. Deep cuts from previous skaters and other imperfections are polished by the Zamboni but not removed entirely. You still feel them under your blades. But skating on a lake…it's as smooth as flying, and if the lake is large, this sense of openness is all the more impactful.

This wine is as smooth as a perfectly frozen lake. There are no rough surfaces or harsh textures to distract you from your enjoyment as you sip, slowly travelling down to the bottom of your glass. While a lot of wines with this grape variety can be harsh, this one is an idyllically smooth experience that you can enjoy regardless of the weather conditions.

RED

You could sip this
out of a salad bowl,
and it would still
taste fantastic.

PENINSULA RIDGE ESTATES WINERY RESERVE MERITAGE

WINERY PRICE: 🍷 🍷 🍷 🍷
BODY: FULL
SWEETNESS: DRY
ATTITUDE: LIMITLESS

Pair with: Osso bucco, bison burgers, sunsets

There is a big difference between the view from the CN Tower on a clear day compared to a rainy one. You either have to use your imagination or just enjoy the view that you do have, limited as it might be. Yes, that special app with the augmented reality can help you see the landmarks obscured by the clouds, but the experience isn't the same as seeing them for yourself. Taking in the view of the city and the lake—along with the vineyards on the other side, of course—from that vantage point is an experience that requires clear skies.

When a wine is limitless, you can tell. Nothing gets in the way of the aromas or flavours. It's like having a direct view to the grapes that went into making it. There are no tricks to hide the flavours of these beautifully grown and ripened grapes. No special stemware or varietal-specific wineglass will dull the way this wine shines. You could sip this out of a salad bowl, and it would still taste fantastic.

How does one experience a limitless wine? Sipsters know that you have to take your time. Put your nose in the glass and take a sniff. Smell that? And that? And maybe that? Take a sip and enjoy. Have some food. Talk a little bit. Repeat. Notice how the things that you smell and taste shift over time. Has the wine changed? Have you? Maybe just a little. You'll learn more with every sip.

This is truly a CN Tower experience, minus the line and the sardine-tight elevator ride to the top.

RED

The beats are going strong, and the audience bounces along with them.

QUEENSTON MILE VINEYARD PINOT NOIR

WINERY PRICE: 🍷 🍷 🍷 🍷
BODY: MEDIUM
SWEETNESS: DRY
ATTITUDE: COMPLEX

Pair with: Truffle perogies, grilled sausages, cold winter nights

---

Like an older sibling who knows jiu jitsu, this wine will kick your ass, but in a familial way that feels relatively safe. It's a Pinot Noir that knows it's a Pinot Noir. It also knows exactly how good it is.

The aromas are the first sign of its greatness. They jump out of the glass and *boop* your nose. There are a lot of them, and they keep you guessing each time you put your nose to the glass. Sniff. *Boop*. Repeat and feel the love.

When you finally take a sip, a set of complex flavours rush you, but you know better than to rush yourself. This combination will take some time to reconcile. Much like the flavours, this wine has texture in abundance. It's velvety smooth, with tannins that keep everything together, like a great drummer in a band. The drummer keeps everything on track. The beats are going strong, and the audience bounces along with them.

That's what this wine does. It rules the groove. Especially if that drummer is someone's older sibling who knows jiu jitsu.

RED

The other tables at the restaurant may have wine, but they don't have *this* wine.

RENNIE ESTATE WINERY
OBSIDIAN CABERNET SAUVIGNON

WINERY PRICE: 🍷 🍷 🍷 🍷 🍷
BODY: FULL
SWEETNESS: DRY
ATTITUDE: LUXURIOUS

Pair with: Braised beef short ribs, Irish lamb stew, private jets

Sipping this wine at a restaurant while watching the other patrons is like standing by a private jet as the people across the tarmac file into a commercial flight. You know you're experiencing something similar, but you're experiencing it in a far more luxurious way. The other tables at the restaurant may have wine, but they don't have *this* wine. Sucks to be them.

For those of us who don't experience luxury on a daily basis, it's a special treat. Getting bumped up to first class or splurging on a highly rated hotel has a decadence that can make you feel instantly comfortable. After a long day of travelling, sliding into a bed that has sheets with crazy thread counts makes you appreciate this luxury even more. The world is amazing when you're surrounded by the best of the best. Not all of us can experience this every day, and if you can, you probably know how lucky you are.

This is first-class wine. Its ultra-smooth, refined texture makes you do a double take. Is this real? Am I really feeling a liquid this silky smooth in my mouth? Oh my...Is this really a wine from Ontario? From Canada?

Yes, and yes. Luxury is all around you when you sip this wine.

RED

But, blessedly, there are times when the plan is having no plan at all.

ROSEHALL RUN
CHERRYWOOD PINOT NOIR

WINERY PRICE: 🍷 🍷 🍷 🍷
BODY: MEDIUM
SWEETNESS: DRY
ATTITUDE: CASUAL

Pair with: Mushroom risotto, chicken paninis, no plans

It's good to make plans. Keeping them intact is another story. Some people are great at making plans but less skilled at sticking to them. Others are great at following through with their plans but not particularly good at coming up with ideas to begin with.

But, blessedly, there are times when the plan is having no plan at all—holidays and vacations where the only thing on the schedule is getting where you need to go. Then it's just precious time off.

This wine was made for these moments. There are no big tannins pushing you to be on time or obtuse flavours that demand particular food pairings. This wine hangs loose and allows you to taste the casual freedom of being on a holiday with no set schedule. And that feeling renews with every sip.

There's no rush to finish your glass. Take your time! Enjoy the moment.

Sipster's Tip: Chilling this wine slightly, half an hour in the fridge prior to opening it, will make this a refreshing summer red.

Every social group
has its pillar
of assembly.

ROSEWOOD "NIGHT MOVES" GAMAY

WINERY PRICE: 🍷 🍷 🍷 🍷
BODY: MEDIUM
SWEETNESS: DRY
ATTITUDE: SOCIABLE

Pair with: Rye-braised chicken with tarragon, spicy pizzas, elegant soirees

---

I once had a customer, at a wine store where I worked, who complained vociferously about having people over at his house all of the time. "I don't get it. Seems like every weekend there are people around the pool, drinking my wine and using the barbecue."

"Maybe if you didn't have the pool and the wine and the barbeque?" I offered, half paying attention while working.

"Well, what fun would that be?" he replied.

Every social group has its pillar of assembly, that one person who has the coolest place with the coolest things (the dream kitchen, the home theatre, the patio set-up, etc.). Intentionally or not, these people become the social vortexes of their groups.

Sipsters often embody that bright centre; wine is a highly social beverage, and a visit to a sipster's home may draw people in with the promise of amazing new taste experiences. But only very special wines can draw people to them. These are the wines that stand out at receptions, appearing in everyone's Instagram reels, eliciting exclamations—*This is so good!*—and acting as a conversational hook between people who have never met.

This Gamay is one of those wines. It has its own gravitational pull. The mysteriously brooding bottle is attractive enough, but once your guests taste it, they may find even more reasons to stay longer.

RED

It's almost like simple, old pesto isn't considered as serious as other sauces.

SOUTHBROOK GAMAY

WINERY PRICE: 🍷 🍷 🍷 🍷
BODY: LIGHT
SWEETNESS: DRY
ATTITUDE: CORDIAL

Pair with: Pasta with fresh pesto, Genoa salami, west coast swing dancing

---

There's something about pesto that just makes the tastebuds dance. If flavours were colours, pesto would be decidedly green—not because most pestos are based on green herbs but because of the pronounced herbal flavours. Sundried tomato pesto can also make the tastebuds cha-cha. However it's made, when pesto is done right, it has a beautifully light flavour with an amazingly broad depth. When the flavours and textures of pine nuts, oil, cheese, and those magical basil leaves combine in the perfect proportions, it feels like you're tasting in three dimensions.

Unfortunately, pesto isn't always treated with the same enthusiasm that other forms of pasta coatings enjoy. Alfredos, béchamels, and carbonaras offer up luscious creamy bases while the mighty tomato dominates everything from arrabiata to vodka sauces. It's almost like simple, old pesto isn't considered as serious as other sauces.

Likewise, the Gamay grape and the often light- to medium-bodied wines it produces are relegated to the same echelon of wine that pesto is to pasta sauces. It doesn't have the tannic *zing* of Cabernet Sauvignon or the powerful *oomph* of Merlot, but it offers a surprising amount of depth, even as a lighter wine. Gamay, like pesto, made properly with care and attention, can grab you by the taste buds and take you on a memorable adventure. Maybe even to your new happy place.

RED

No annoying little
paper gift bag
required.

TRIUS ESTATES RED THE ICON

WINERY PRICE: 🍷 🍷 🍷
BODY: FULL
SWEETNESS: DRY
ATTITUDE: OVERACHIEVING

Pair with: Grilled striploin, lamb skewers, dinner with the future in-laws

---

There are times when you want to impress—a client, a new co-worker, or the parents you're meeting for the first time. Dressing up gives us a little boost of confidence, making it a perfect place to start. You can also bring some wine along to show off a little. But do you know enough about wine? A lot of people don't feel confident enough in their choices to attempt this.

This is where the Trius Red The Icon shines. This wine isn't only dressed to impress, but it also tastes far better than you might expect given its price point. The bottle is beautifully tall and slender, unlike any other bottle available. Those who shop by the label (even sipsters do this sometimes) will find this wine already wearing its best formal attire. No annoying little paper gift bag required.

So it looks great. Who cares? What about the taste? This is where this wine goes beyond cellar window dressing. It's a solid wine from cork to punt and over-delivers on everything promised by its price.

❑ CHÂTEAU DES CHARMES VIDAL ICEWINE   119

❑ LAKEVIEW CELLARS VIDAL ICEWINE   121

❑ MAGNOTTA CABERNET FRANC ICEWINE   123

❑ REIF ESTATE WINERY VIDAL ICEWINE   125

❑ STONEHOUSE VINEYARD 1793   127

DESSERT WINES

Dessert wines are a special category that encompass-es fortified wines, late harvest wines, and Icewines. They range from being a little sweet to OMG sweet (*luscious* is the accepted descriptor in some traditional tasting methods). But here's the weird thing about sweet wines: despite their decadence, nobody really knows what to do with them. We drink pop with our burgers while sitting in movie theatres. Sweet stuff is everywhere. So why the hesitation with sweet wines?

Perhaps this hesitation arises from the fact that some sweet wines have massive amounts of sugar compound-ed with a significant amount of alcohol (*lots* of alco-hol in the case of fortified wines). *Woah now*, you may think. *That's too much. We don't want a wicked head-ache tomorrow!*

The secret to dessert wines is this: you don't have to drink the whole bottle. In fact, that shouldn't be the goal. One night, at the end of a party, a friend and I decided to polish off the last half of a bottle of Icewine. Though it wasn't a lot of wine, it was enough sugar to qualify it as an upper. I spent the night in bed extremely tired, my eyes bolted open from the sugar rush, unable to get to sleep until 4 AM.

Sweet wines will last a long time after they've been opened, so there's no need to rush. They aren't dry table wines, so stop trying to drink them the same way. Take your time.

I always wondered what made people want to cook or bake for others.

CHÂTEAU DES CHARMES VIDAL ICEWINE

WINERY PRICE: 🍷 🍷 🍷
BODY: FULL
SWEETNESS: LUSCIOUS
ATTITUDE: ARROOOOGAH!

Pair with: Peach pies, cheesecake, spending quality time with someone special

Friend: *Sniff*
Friend: *Wow*!
Friend: *Sniff*
Friend: Oh man!
Friend: *Sip*
Friend: I *love* this!
Friend: *Sip*
Friend: Wow, uh, oh my ...
Friend: *Deep breaths*
Me: ... So, you like it, then?
Friend: *Smiling a little* Oh yeah, it's so good ...

As an adult, I understand things a little better than I did when I was younger (or at least I think I do). I always wondered what made people want to cook or bake for others. Why do people become chefs? Other than out of necessity, how do parents derive any sense of joy from cooking for their families?

Now, I get it. Seeing the joyous reactions of the people who eat your culinary creations is enough. Pouring this wine after a long meal and getting a similar reaction is priceless.

If grapevines have a sense of humour, it's a slightly ironic one.

LAKEVIEW CELLARS VIDAL ICEWINE

WINERY PRICE: 🍷 🍷 🍷
BODY: FULL
SWEETNESS: SWEET
ATTITUDE: HUMOROUS

Pair with: Penang prawn curry, peach galette, weekends away

The aromas and flavours of this wine are so different from the season in which it was created that one begins to think that grapevines have a crazy sense of humour.

Winter is not a particularly aromatic season. Everything is cold and frosty, and none of the smells are particularly interesting. True, there's the frosty aroma of ice being scraped off a windshield, but generally, aromas become more muted as the temperature lowers. Sipsters know this from experiencing wines served at the wrong temperature, at restaurants and even in their own homes. Chill a Chardonnay too much and you'll wonder after a couple of sniffs how it could possibly be worth more than $30. But when it warms up a little, it suddenly becomes very expressive.

If grapevines have a sense of humour, it's a slightly ironic one. Grapevines that are subjected to the rigours of having their grapes frozen before harvest are experts in a uniquely humorous brand of irony. During harvest, they make it abundantly clear that they'd rather be off sunning themselves in Mexico and imbue the resulting Icewine with aromas from just about every known tropical fruit simply to taunt us. It can only be the irony of the vines themselves that gives Icewine so many beautiful, summery, fresh fruit aromas. Why does that happen?

As soon as you sip this Icewine, the answer is clear: Who cares? Enjoy those beautiful tropical flavours and revel in the irony.

They don't play games
by trying to act all
casual and cautious.

MAGNOTTA CABERNET FRANC ICEWINE

WINERY PRICE: 🍷🍷🍷🍷🍷
BODY: FULL
SWEETNESS: LUSCIOUS
ATTITUDE: SHY

Pair with: Blue cheeses, roast beef with a sweet cherry glaze, late-night text conversations

Icewines can be very forward about who they are. They are sweet. They are unctuous. They are intense. They don't play games by trying to act all casual and cautious, responding to your inquiries with two-word sentences and then staring off into the smouldering sunset during the dessert course. They can't hide the fact that they're sweet. They're dressed up in thin little Bellissima bottles and usually cost a lot more than regular wines. They are always in a different part of the wine store—in plain sight but not always noticed.

Pairing an Icewine with a wine lover can be difficult. Even hardcore sipsters aren't always sure when to invite an Icewine to the party. *What if it's too sweet for the dessert? Will everyone like it as much as I do? Will there be enough for everyone in that small bottle?* Not everyone can appreciate what an Icewine has to offer, despite the fact that Icewine is fairly approachable. Everyone likes sweet things even if they don't take time to appreciate all the nuances.

This Icewine is defined by its reserved sensitivity. Not every wine drinker appreciates its forward flavours and sweetness. But if they can see past these elements to the true essence of this wine (it's a wine, not a super-sweet juice), they will be rewarded. It's shy, and a multitude of aromas are hidden because so many people drink it too cold. It lacks recognition because sweetness makes us rush toward instant gratification.

Take the time to notice the nuances of this wine. You will be rewarded with a very special experience.

If you're looking for a wine that cannot be adequately described with few words, this is the one.

REIF ESTATE WINERY VIDAL ICEWINE

WINERY PRICE: 🍷 🍷 🍷
BODY: FULL
SWEETNESS: LUSCIOUS
ATTITUDE: POETIC

Pair with: Crème brûlée, fruit dipped in chocolate, cuddling with someone special under a blanket

Albert Einstein is often credited with a quote which states that things should be said as simply as possible, but no simpler. This is great advice for communicating important facts and events, but does it really capture our sensory experiences as humans? If you look outside at a park lined with trees, is describing it all as "green space" enough? Is that all it is? You may need to find more descriptors to really capture the experience of looking out at that park. Are there trails? Pathways? A playground? An off-leash dog park? An amphitheatre? A river or stream?

Some things don't require many words. *Grey* is probably a universally acceptable descriptor for a parking lot. "Grey with lines" would work too. So, is it better if a wine requires two words or two paragraphs to describe? That depends on what you're looking for and the occasion on which you plan to enjoy it.

If you're looking for a wine that cannot be adequately described with few words, this is the one. This wine says everything in a complex way. There are loads of intriguing aromas and flavours that could have been clearly communicated without the flourishes, but those flourishes make it a unique and amazing experience to taste.

There will be giggles.
There will be smiles.

STONEHOUSE VINEYARD 1793

WINERY PRICE: ♈ ♈ ♈
BODY: MEDIUM
SWEETNESS: SWEET
ATTITUDE: CARNIVAL RIDE

Pair with: Strong cheeses, jerk-seasoned lamb chops, an energetic playlist

Tasting this wine is a ride. A carnival ride. One sniff and you're off on a tilt-a-whirl of aromas, complete with flashing lights and cheeky circus music. Up and down. Around and around. Whipping by occasionally. There will be giggles. There will be smiles. You're doing something completely ridiculous and having fun with the special people who've joined you on this trip. It's wonderfully silly and worth remembering for many years to come.

When the ride is over, you may seek out another one. Some people want the high-octane rides that throw you through the air, hang you upside down, or stick you to a wall. Others prefer the medium-duty wooden roller coasters or the rocking pirate ship. Even these are too much for some, who favour the bumper cars and the ubiquitous teacup ride. Regardless of tastes, the carnival has something for everyone.

There is nothing normal about this beautiful fortified wine, and it's immediately appealing on multiple levels. There's something for you to enjoy, whether it be the beautiful aromas, the intense and appealing flavours, or the extraordinarily smooth texture.

Don't forget to strap yourself in.

SIPSTERS' CODE OF CONDUCT

As sipsters, we acknowledge that we are all individuals with unique taste preferences. Nobody is more of an expert on the way you enjoy wine than you are. Hence I have drafted a new Sipsters' Code of Conduct for enjoying wine.

Share your wines, even the special bottles. If someone is interested in a wine, they will likely appreciate it as well. Enjoying something fantastic together is what being a sipster is all about.

You do not know everything about wine, and you never will. Remember in college when your friends asked you wine questions because you were the "wine expert" in the group? Looking back, how much do you think you knew then? Have you learned more since? Yeah, thought so.

Share your knowledge when it is appropriate. Nobody likes a know-it-all, but people do appreciate help when they need it. Knowing the difference is key to being a sipster.

Do not disparage wines that you don't like. All wine, no matter the quality level, could be someone's favourite bottle.

Enjoy the wine you're with. Never miss the opportunity to enjoy the pleasures of experiencing wine.

SIPSTER'S GUIDE TO PERFECT PAIRINGS

Wine pairings. If you enter that term into your favourite search engine, the results will probably all be about pairing your wine with *food*. There will be pairing suggestions from well-known wine writers, wine magazines, and maybe a food blog or three. Whole books and college courses consider this subject and the science behind it. It's fascinating for people like me who enjoy knowing why something works.

But sipsters know something that most of those wine books and classes don't seriously consider: wine doesn't have to be paired with food alone. The biggest factor in a good wine pairing is the environment, the context. Good restauranteurs know this and work to create the right atmosphere for their clients. But, even while enjoying wine at home, sipsters understand that a truly fantastic wine pairing involves more than just the food on the table.

It's where you are and who you're with. Simply put, it's all about companionship and context. Yes, it's nice to have an elegant table, a beautiful sunset, a picnic blanket, and soul-stirring music. Yes, it's nice to be in conversation with amazing company. You can enjoy all these elements, but if the wine doesn't match the situation, it's all for nought. The wine won't be a valued part of the experience and could even be wasted.

If this seems difficult to quantify, it is. The attitude of the wine needs to match the context, which includes not just the food, but the place and the people as well. Some wines have a lot to say. They are complex, with many aromas, flavours, and textures, all of which can change over time as you swirl the glass. Appreciating this kind of wine takes time and may be distracting in a mismatched context—your mind starts to stray from the conversation because of the wine, or you're so wrapped up in the conversation that you don't even notice the extraordinary flavours as you sip.

I have always found it irritating when a great Champagne is served as a reception wine. It feels like a waste, a distraction. It is difficult to give the wine your full attention because the occasion itself demands so much attention. Focusing on the nuances of a beautiful Champagne are almost impossible in a crowded and noisy room. Did she say that she got a new job? Wow, that tuxedo looks fantastic. Oh look—canapés! The context and the wine are mismatched. A more simple Prosecco or an inexpensive Cava, both of which are far more accessible wines, would fit in this crowded situation much better. Perhaps this is why sparkling wines, in general, are treated as frivolously extravagant, rather than as proper wines to be served with traditional meal courses.

If the wine is busy and complex, find a low-key situation where it can be appreciated without distraction. If the wine is simple, it can enhance a situation that is already full of distractions, like a reception.

Some wines are special. If a wine is special for some reason (such as being aged or rare), find an equally special occasion to open it—a family celebration, a graduation, an engagement announcement, or to celebrate a new addition to the family. These are special life events around which families gather for celebratory meals and commemorative toasts. Everyone settles around the beautifully set table to eat a meal that has taken all afternoon to prepare, and then your dad or father-in-law uncorks a bottle of wine he made from a wine kit in the basement last year. Cue the record scratch. Something is very wrong with this wine in this context.

Kit wines can be delicious, of course, providing good value for the money. But they are never going to be a *special* bottle of wine. Monetary value aside—the price per bottle of a kit wine could be between $4 and $10—the specialness of kit-wine is diminished by the fact that there are 29 identical bottles in the back of a closet somewhere.

A special wine can be expensive, but it doesn't have to be. A wine can be special because it was the first wine that you and your partner purchased together. Or you visited the winery years ago, bought three bottles, and this is the last one that you have. Or maybe you went to Italy five years ago and tasted this wine on your trip but only had room in your luggage to bring back a single bottle. Those are all special bottles to you. Share them with special people at special times.

Some wines set the mood. You can use wine to set the mood, even before you open the bottle. But remember that wines can also distract or—worse—ruin the mood entirely. Does a dayglow yellow label on a bottle of white wine chilling in the fridge scream romance? Perhaps for some, but maybe there are better options.

You can build excitement by displaying wines at a party. Walking into a room with 10 different vintages of the same wine arranged on the table or sideboard really builds the anticipation of trying them all. Bringing out a bottle with a colourful or innovative label can be a great conversation starter. Just seeing a bottle of white or sparkling wine in a frosty ice bucket builds anticipation. Restaurants use these techniques all the time. Some of them have wines displayed on racks as you arrive or along a wall in their main seating area. The standard wine service, with the presentation ritual (when the sommelier or waiter shows it to the host and then opens it at the table in front of everyone) is also a technique for creating excitement.

If it's a casual party, the wines may all be clustered on a table. Maybe there are corkscrews scattered around to encourage people to open whatever they find interesting. More formal or sombre gatherings may require less display; boisterous, colourful labels may not be appropriate in these situations. As for that romantic dinner for two, a bottle without an attention-grabbing label is best. Your gaze should never be distracted by anything more colourful than the eyes of the person you're connecting with.

GENERAL TOURING INFORMATION

Wine touring in Ontario has exploded over the past 20 years. Most wineries have wine shops and all of them are eager to help you learn about the wines they produce.

Wine touring is unique; no other agricultural industry does touring on such a wide scale. Agri-tourism is available wherever there are eager farmers willing to share with the public information about what they do. It's a great way for urban dwellers to learn about where their food comes from and an important way to create a localized market to encourage food security.

However, only wine touring has its own organized infrastructure, such as wine routes (maps, highway signs, etc.) and tour companies to take visitors safely to and from a selection of wineries. When I lived on Prince Edward Island, I never saw signs for potato touring, or any companies willing to take me to visit potato growers. There were no potato tastings or festivals dedicated to potatoes from different parts of the province. I have not yet found any discussions online or books on the subject of pommes de terroir. Append any other agricultural product to the word *touring*, and suddenly it looks silly.

You can go on a "wine tour" simply by travelling to a selection of different wineries on your own. You can also hire a wine tour company, where a professional driver can take you and 24 of your besties in a limousine or small bus to a series of wineries. If the winery chooses to offer them, you can go on a guided tour like that of any tourist destination. Some wineries have self-guided tours. "Wine touring" encompasses all of these different possibilities. However you plan to get to the wineries, there are a few things to consider when choosing where to go and how to get the most out of your experience.

Know what to wear. Dress for comfort. You might look amazing in those heels, but are you going to be comfortable walking in and out of each winery and standing at five different tasting bars over the next five hours?

Know what not to wear. Perfume, hairspray, and or any strong cologne, no matter how fashionable, should all be avoided. If you walk into a wine shop wearing a heavy scent, you'll get noticed for all the wrong reasons. You'd stand out less wearing a pink sombrero and flippers. No amount of social distancing or N95 masks will blunt it. Your cologne or perfume may smell fine to you (you may even be nose-blind to it), but it can negatively alter other customers' experiences of the wines they've come to taste. You will absolutely be made fun of after you leave. Guaranteed.

Protect your wine from heat. This takes some planning, but it's critically important, especially in the summer when a parked car can heat up in an instant. Consider bringing a cooler or lots of blankets to insulate your wine boxes. The coolest part of a vehicle is usually on the floor of the back seat, and a heavy blanket will protect your wine from direct sunlight best there. Do not use the trunk or the box of a pickup, both of which are outside air-conditioning zones. You may also consider bringing your wine inside each winery as you go. This isn't convenient, but if you're planning to purchase only a few bottles, it is completely acceptable. If you are buying cases, consider having them shipped home instead. Most wineries are more than happy to do this.

Explore. Prioritize visiting new wineries. If a winery looks appealing to you, go for it. Follow your nose. Exploring is what wine touring is all about. You may find the most amazing wine you've ever tasted somewhere you never expected.

Love the driver you're with. For everyone's safety, you need a designated driver. If you don't have any volunteers, consider my DD rule: the group must purchase a bottle of wine from each winery and gift it to their DD. This is a great way to include your DD in the tour, and they get to enjoy the wines later.

Set your expectations to stun. The days of visiting 8–10 wineries in one go are over. The old-style standing-room only, cattle-trough tasting experiences are now (thankfully) in the past. The best post-pandemic winery experiences usually involve a comfortable, sit-down tasting that takes a little extra time. Drive times between wineries can be considerable, so it helps to plan your route carefully and spend the day within a single region (say, Niagara Lakeshore). You will have a much better experience overall and get a more realistic sense of the wines, and potentially the wine region as a whole, than ever before. Sure, you won't be able to visit as many wineries in a single day, but your overall experience will be a lot better. Plus, you'll be refreshed enough for a second day of touring.

CONFESSIONS OF A SIPSTER

What makes you such a wine expert anyway? I've been in the industry, working with wine daily, for over 18 years. I've written for a major wine periodical (7 years), produced a podcast about wine in British Columbia (6 years), and wrote a wine blog (about 14 years). I have written and published four other books on wine. I teach the Wine Sales Certificate program at Okanagan College in Penticton, as well as other seminars on food pairing, BC wine history, and sales techniques. If an actual certification is important to you, I have WSET (Wine & Spirit Education Trust) Level 3 and have almost completed my Level 4 diploma. If all that doesn't make me knowledgeable enough about wine, then my professional experience as a cellar hand and in wine sales and marketing makes up the difference.

Did you actually taste all that wine? Yes, I did, but not in the focused way that wines are normally tasted for writing tasting notes. Instead, I did passive tastings and used the wines as I normally would—during meals and occasions where wine is consumed. Afterwards, I would write my full notes as soon as possible.

What do you know about Ontario wine? Aren't you from British Columbia? Actually, I was born in Quebec and lived there until I was twenty-one. BC is the fifth province I've called home. I've been to wineries in all four major wine-producing provinces and have experienced wine from Ontario since 1996. If being from a place is a major qualification for writing about wine, then most wine books can be discounted because they were written by British authors.

So, where are the vintages? Aren't those important? I do not mention anything about a wine's vintage in this book. If a wine is included here, it's because I believe it's a solid performer regardless of the vintage. These wines should be consistently good no matter what year they were produced, meaning that you can continue to seek them out for many years to come, confident that the winery in question produces amazing wines.

CHEERS TO
WONDERFUL PEOPLE

I have many people to thank for this book's existence.

A huge thank you to my sipster crew—Adrienne, Avery, Paul, Kristi, and Greg—who helped me taste an amazing amount of wine and inspired me with phrases and ideas when I was drawing a total blank.

Thank you Annika Betts, Grant Biggs, Mitzi Dandy, Catherine Montgomery, and Ann Sperling for being wonderful sipsters and suggesting new wines to seek out.

Thank you to John Schreiner and Kimberly Hundertmark for going above and beyond to connect me to some of the amazing people in Ontario's wine community.

And thank you to Tori, Kate, Curtis, and Senica at TouchWood for believing that a book like this could work in the first place.

INDEX

A

activity pairing, dessert wines
    and an energetic playlist, 127
    cuddling someone special, 125
    late night text conversations, 123
    spending quality time
        with someone, 119
    weekends away, 121
activity pairing, red wines
    blind tastings, 95
    Bob James's music, 89
    cold winter nights, 105
    completing a long road trip, 85
    debates, 87
    digital detoxes, 97
    dinner with future in-laws, 115
    elegant soirées, 111
    kumbaya, 99
    listening to music, 81
    no plans, 109
    and old rocking chairs, 83
    private jets, 107
    reunions, 91
    snowstorms, 101
    sunsets, 103
    wedding receptions, 93
    West Coast swing dancing, 113
activity pairing, rosé wines
    busy afternoons, 69
    recovering from work week, 77
    swiping right, 75
    watching Formula 1, 71
activity pairing, sparkling wines
    frolicking, 25
    good times, 29
    hot tubs, 27
    impressing a date, 41
    picnics, 23
    reminiscing, 43
activity pairing, white wines
    beach picnic, 45
    a day in the snow, 53
    deep conversations, 55
    enjoying sunshine, 61

    Frank Sinatra, 63
    with friends, 35
    heralding, 51
    listening to 80s vinyl, 37
    before a long weekend, 39
    lunch with friends, 65
    and nostalgia, 49
    puzzles, 57
    reconnecting with friends, 59
    reminiscing, 49
    romantic movies, 33
    stargazing, 47
aggressive tasting, 7
Angels Gate Sparkling Chardonnay, 21
aromatic descriptors, about, 5, 8, 15–16
attitude, about, 15–16, 129
auxerrois
    Oxley Estate
        Winery Auxerrois, 43
    Waupoos Estate
        Winery Auxerrois, 63

B

baco noir, Henry of Pelham
    Baco Noir, 95
behaviour, for sipsters, 128
blanc de noirs, Magnotta Blanc
    de Noirs Sparkling Wine, 27
body
    about, 13–14
body, full, dessert wines
    Château des Charmes
        Vidal Icewine, 119
    Lakeview Cellars Vidal
        Icewine, 121
    Magnotta Cabernet Franc
        Icewine, 123
    Reif Estate Winery Vidal
        Icewine, 125
body, full, red wines
    Peller Estates Private Reserve
        Cabernet Sauvignon, 101
    Peninsula Ridge Estates Winery
        Reserve Meritage, 103

Rennie Estate Winery Obsidian
Cabernet Sauvignon, 107
Trius Estates Red The Icon, 115
body, full, white wines
Queenston Mile Vineyard
Chardonnay, 49
body, light, red wines
Cloudsley Cellars Pinot Noir, 85
Malivoire Farmstead Gamay, 99
Southbrook Gamay, 113
body, light, rosé wines
Mindful Rosé, 69
Revel Cider IBI Apollo Rosé, 75
Southbrook Triomphe
Cabernet Franc Rosé, 77
body, light, sparkling wines
Angels Gate Sparkling
Chardonnay, 21
Château des Charmes Winery
Rosé Sparkling, 23
body, light, white wines
Cave Spring Riesling, 33
KIN Vineyards Chardonnay, 37
Mindful Pinot Grigio, 39
Twenty Bees Pinot Grigio, 59
Vineland Estates Winery
Chardonnay Musqué, 61
Waupoos Estate Winery
Auxerrois, 63
Wayne Gretzky Estates
Sauvignon Blanc, 65
body, medium, dessert wines
Stonehouse Vineyard 1793, 127
body, medium, red wines
Closson Chase Churchside
Pinot Noir, 83
Domaine Queylus Réserve du
Domaine Pinot Noir, 87
EastDell Cabernet Franc, 89
Featherstone Cabernet Franc, 91
Flat Rock Cellars Gravity
Pinot Noir, 93
Henry of Pelham Baco Noir, 95
LOLA Cabernet Sauvignon/
Cabernet Franc, 97
Queenston Mile Vineyard
Pinot Noir, 105
Rosehall Run Cherrywood
Pinot Noir, 109
Rosewood "Night Moves"
Gamay, 111

16 Mile Cellar Rebel Pinot
Noir Gamay, 81
body, medium, rosé wines
Oxley Estate Winery Cab
Syrah Rosé, 71
Paradise Grapevine Vin de Soif
Gamay & Zweigelt, 73
body, medium, sparkling wines
Kew Vineyards Pinot
Meunier Sparkling, 25
Magnotta Blanc de Noirs
Sparkling Wine, 27
Peller Estates Ice Cuvée
Classic, 29
body, medium, white wines
Flat Rock Cellars Nadja's
Vineyard Riesling, 35
On Seven the Pursuit
Chardonnay, 41
Oxley Estate Winery
Auxerrois, 43
Paradise Grapevine Golden
Hour, 45
Peninsula Ridge Estates Winery
Sauvignon Blanc, 47
Reif Estate Winery Reserve
Pinot Grigio, 51
Rosewood Cellars Legacy
Spiced Mead, 53
Sue-Ann Staff Estate Winery
Riesling, 55
Trail Estate Winery
Chardonnay, 57
Bosker, Bianca, 7, 9

C

cabernet franc
EastDell Cabernet Franc, 89
Featherstone Cabernet Franc, 91
LOLA Cabernet Sauvignon/
Cabernet Franc, 97
Magnotta Cabernet Franc
Icewine, 123
Southbrook Triomphe
Cabernet Franc Rosé, 77
cabernet sauvignon
LOLA Cabernet Sauvignon/
Cabernet Franc, 97
Peller Estates Private Reserve
Cabernet Sauvignon, 101
Rennie Estate Winery Obsidian
Cabernet Sauvignon, 107

cabernet syrah
  Oxley Estate Winery Cab
    Syrah Rosé, 71
Canadian wines, point scores for, 10
Cave Spring Riesling, 33
chardonnay
  about, 121
  Angels Gate Sparkling
    Chardonnay, 21
  KIN Vineyards Chardonnay, 37
  On Seven the Pursuit
    Chardonnay, 41
  Queenston Mile Vineyard
    Chardonnay, 49
  Trail Estate Winery
    Chardonnay, 57
chardonnay musqué
  Vineland Estates Winery
    Chardonnay Musqué, 61
Château des Charmes Vidal Icewine, 119
Château des Charmes Winery Rosé
  Sparkling, 23
Closson Chase Churchside Pinot Noir,
  83
clothing, for touring, 133
Cloudsley Cellars Pinot Noir, 85
code of conduct, 128
communication, about wine
  descriptors, about, 5, 15–16
  tasting notes, 6, 7–8, 9
  Wine Aroma Wheel, 8
Cork Dork (Bosker), 7, 9

D
designated driver, using, 133
dessert wines
  about, 117
  Château des Charmes
    Vidal Icewine, 119
  Lakeview Cellars Vidal
    Icewine, 121
  Magnotta Cabernet Franc
    Icewine, 123
  Reif Estate Winery Vidal
    Icewine, 125
  Stonehouse Vineyard 1793, 127
Domaine Queylus Réserve du
  Domaine Pinot Noir, 87

E
EastDell Cabernet Franc, 89
Emandare Vineyard, 12

experiences, wine, 11, 12
experiencing wine
  initially, 4
  limitations of descriptors, 5
  pairing, 3, 15–16, 129–131
  taste, influences on, 6–7
  tasting notes, usefulness of, 6

F
Featherstone Cabernet Franc, 91
Flat Rock Cellars Gravity Pinot Noir, 93
Flat Rock Cellars Nadja's Vineyard
  Riesling, 35
food pairing, about, 16, 73, 129
food pairing, dessert wines
  beef, 123
  cheese, 123, 127
  desserts, 119, 121, 125
  lamb, 127
  seafood, 121
food pairing, red wines
  beef, 91, 95, 99, 101, 103, 107, 115
  bison, 103
  charcuterie, 87, 113
  cheese, 83, 85, 87
  chicken, 81, 97, 109, 111
  duck, 93
  lamb, 101, 107, 115
  olives, 95
  pasta, 97, 113
  perogies, 105
  pizza, 89, 111
  pork, 81, 89
  risotto, 93, 109
  salads, 85, 99
  sausages, 97, 105
  tapenades, 83
food pairing, rosé wines
  chicken, 69
  fajitas, 75
  pizza, 75
  pork, 71
  snacks, 69, 77
  turkey, 71
food pairing, sparkling wines
  canapés, 21
  cheese, 25, 27, 29
  chicken, 23, 41
  desserts, 21, 25
  fish, 41
  salads, 23, 43
  seafood, 27

spicy food, 29
vegetables, 43
food pairing, white wines
charcuterie, 39
cheese, 45, 65
chicken, 33, 61
chowder, 49, 57
desserts, 53
fish, 35, 37, 49, 51, 63
ham, 35
nuts, 53
pizza, 37, 47, 57
pork, 55
salads, 39, 51, 59, 65
seafood, 33, 47, 57, 59, 61
vegetables, 55, 63

G

gamay
about, 113
Malivoire Farmstead Gamay, 99
Paradise Grapevine Vin de Soif
Gamay & Zweigelt, 73
Rosewood "Night Moves"
Gamay, 111
16 Mile Cellar Rebel Pinot
Noir Gamay, 81
Southbrook Gamay, 113

H

heat, protecting wine from, 133
Henry of Pelham Baco Noir, 95

I

icewine
Château des Charmes
Vidal Icewine, 119
Lakeview Cellars Vidal
Icewine, 121
Magnotta Cabernet Franc
Icewine, 123
point scores for, 10
Reif Estate Winery Vidal
Icewine, 125
influencers, effect of, 2

K

Kew Vineyards Pinot Meunier
Sparkling, 25
KIN Vineyards Chardonnay, 37
kit wines, 130–131

L

Lakeview Cellars Vidal Icewine, 121
LOLA Cabernet Sauvignon /
Cabernet Franc, 97
luscious (sweetness), 117

M

Magnotta Blanc de Noirs
Sparkling Wine, 27
Magnotta Cabernet Franc Icewine, 123
Malivoire Farmstead Gamay, 99
mead, Rosewood Cellars Legacy
Spiced Mead, 53
meritage, Peninsula Ridge Estates
Winery Reserve Meritage, 103
Mindful Pinot Grigio, 39
Mindful Rosé, 69
monofacture, 4, 5
mood, pairing wine with, 131

N

Nierychlo, Mike and Robin, 12
Noble, Ann, 8

O

off-dry, about, 15
On Seven the Pursuit Chardonnay, 41
Ottawa wine region, 37
Oxley Estate Winery Auxerrois, 43
Oxley Estate Winery Cab Syrah Rosé, 71

P

pairing wine
about, 16, 73, 129
with attitude, 129
with context, 16, 129, 130–131
with food, 73 (*see also* food
pairing, dessert wines; food
pairing, red wines; food
pairing, rosé wines; food
pairing, sparkling wines;
food pairing, white wines)
with mood, 131
Paradise Grapevine Golden Hour, 45
Paradise Grapevine Vin de Soif Gamay
& Zweigelt, 73
Parker, Robert, 9
Peller Estates Ice Cuvée Classic, 29
Peller Estates Private Reserve Cabernet
Sauvignon, 101
Peninsula Ridge Estates Winery Reserve
Meritage, 103

Peninsula Ridge Estates Winery
  Sauvignon Blanc, 47
picnics, 23
pinot grigio
  Mindful Pinot Grigio, 39
  Reif Estate Winery Reserve
    Pinot Grigio, 51
  Twenty Bees Pinot Grigio, 59
pinot meunier
  Kew Vineyards Pinot Meunier
    Sparkling, 25
pinot noir
  Closson Chase Churchside
    Pinot Noir, 83
  Cloudsley Cellars Pinot Noir, 85
  Domaine Queylus Réserve du
    Domaine Pinot Noir, 87
  Flat Rock Cellars Gravity
    Pinot Noir, 93
  Queenston Mile Vineyard
    Pinot Noir, 105
  Rosehall Run Cherrywood
    Pinot Noir, 109
  16 Mile Cellar Rebel Pinot
    Noir Gamay, 81
Plato, on smell, 8
point scores, system of, 9–11
presentation, 131
price, $10-$20
  Cave Spring Riesling, 33
  Henry of Pelham Baco Noir, 95
  LOLA Cabernet Sauvignon/
    Cabernet Franc, 97
  Mindful Pinot Grigio, 39
  Mindful Rosé, 69
  Oxley Estate Winery Cab
    Syrah Rosé, 71
  Twenty Bees Pinot Grigio, 59
  Vineland Estates Winery
    Chardonnay Musqué, 61
  Wayne Gretzky Estates
    Sauvignon Blanc, 65
price, $20-$30
  Angels Gate Sparkling
    Chardonnay, 21
  Château des Charmes Vidal
    Icewine, 119
  EastDell Cabernet Franc, 89
  Featherstone Cabernet Franc, 91
  Kew Vineyards Pinot Meunier
    Sparkling, 25
  KIN Vineyards Chardonnay, 37

Lakeview Cellars Vidal
  Icewine, 121
Magnotta Blanc de Noirs
  Sparkling Wine, 27
Malivoire Farmstead Gamay, 99
Oxley Estate Winery Auxerrois,
  43
Peller Estates Private Reserve
  Cabernet Sauvignon, 101
Peninsula Ridge Estates Winery
  Sauvignon Blanc, 47
Reif Estate Winery Reserve
  Pinot Grigio, 51
Reif Estate Winery Vidal
  Icewine, 125
Revel Cider IBI Apollo Rosé, 75
Rosewood Cellars Legacy Spiced
  Mead, 53
16 Mile Cellar Rebel Pinot Noir
  Gamay, 81
Southbrook Triomphe Cabernet
  Franc Rosé, 77
Stonehouse Vineyard 1793, 127
Sue-Ann Staff Estate Winery
  Riesling, 55
Trius Estates Red The Icon, 115
Waupoos Estate Winery
  Auxerrois, 63
price, $30-$40
  Château des Charmes Winery
    Rosé Sparkling, 23
  Cloudsley Cellars Pinot Noir, 85
  Flat Rock Cellars Nadja's
    Vineyard Riesling, 35
  Paradise Grapevine Golden
    Hour, 45
  Paradise Grapevine Vin de Soif
    Gamay & Zweigelt, 73
  Peller Estates Ice Cuvée
    Classic, 29
  Peninsula Ridge Estates Winery
    Reserve Meritage, 103
  Queenston Mile Vineyard
    Chardonnay, 49
  Rosehall Run Cherrywood
    Pinot Noir, 109
  Rosewood "Night Moves"
    Gamay, 111
  Southbrook Gamay, 113
price, $40-$50
  Closson Chase Churchside
    Pinot Noir, 83

Domaine Queylus Réserve du
    Domaine Pinot Noir, 87
Flat Rock Cellars Gravity
    Pinot Noir, 93
Magnotta Cabernet Franc
    Icewine, 123
On Seven the Pursuit
    Chardonnay, 41
Queenston Mile Vineyard
    Pinot Noir, 105
Rennie Estate Winery Obsidian
    Cabernet Sauvignon, 107
Trail Estate Winery
    Chardonnay, 57
price, about, 13–14

Q

Queenston Mile Vineyard
    Chardonnay, 49
Queenston Mile Vineyard
    Pinot Noir, 105

R

Reading Between the Wines (Theise), 7
red wines
    about, 79
    Closson Chase Churchside
        Pinot Noir, 83
    Cloudsley Cellars Pinot Noir, 85
    Domaine Queylus Réserve Du
        Domaine Pinot Noir, 87
    EastDell Cabernet Franc, 89
    Featherstone Cabernet Franc, 91
    Flat Rock Cellars Gravity
        Pinot Noir, 93
    Henry of Pelham Baco Noir, 95
    LOLA Cabernet Sauvignon/
        Cabernet Franc, 97
    Malivoire Farmstead Gamay, 99
    Peller Estates Private Reserve
        Cabernet Sauvignon, 101
    Peninsula Ridge Estates Winery
        Reserve Meritage, 103
    Queenston Mile Vineyard
        Pinot Noir, 105
    Rennie Estate Winery Obsidian
        Cabernet Sauvignon, 107
    Rosehall Run Cherrywood
        Pinot Noir, 109
    Rosewood "Night Moves"
        Gamay, 111
    16 Mile Cellar Rebel Pinot

Noir Gamay, 81
    Southbrook Gamay, 113
    Trius Estates Red The Icon, 115
Reif Estate Winery Reserve
    Pinot Grigio, 51
Reif Estate Winery Vidal Icewine, 125
Rennie Estate Winery Obsidian
    Cabernet Sauvignon, 107
Revel Cider IBI Apollo Rosé, 75
riesling
    Cave Spring Riesling, 33
    Flat Rock Cellars Nadja's
        Vineyard Riesling, 35
    Paradise Grapevine
        Golden Hour, 45
    Sue-Ann Staff Estate Winery
        Riesling, 55
Rosehall Run Cherrywood
    Pinot Noir, 109
rosé wines
about, 67
    Château des Charmes Winery
        Rosé Sparkling, 23
    Mindful Rosé, 69
    Oxley Estate Winery Cab
        Syrah Rosé, 71
    Paradise Grapevine Vin de Soif
        Gamay & Zweigelt, 73
    Revel Cider IBI Apollo Rosé, 75
    Southbrook Triomphe Cabernet
        Franc Rosé, 77
Rosewood Cellars Legacy
    Spiced Mead, 53
Rosewood "Night Moves" Gamay, 111

S

sauvignon blanc
    Peninsula Ridge Estates Winery
        Sauvignon Blanc, 47
    Wayne Gretzky Estates
        Sauvignon Blanc, 65
scent, wearing on tours, 133
Sideways, 35
sipster
    definition, 2
    philosophy, 3
*The Sipster's Pocket Guide to 50 Must-Try
    Ontario Wines*
    information presented, 13–14
    purpose of book, 6
    wine tasting protocol used, 13

16 Mile Cellar Rebel Pinot Noir
Gamay, 81
smell
describing, 8
Plato on, 8
relationship to taste, 8–9
sense of, 8
Southbrook Gamay, 113
Southbrook Triomphe Cabernet
Franc Rosé, 77
sparkling wines
about, 19
Angels Gate Sparkling
Chardonnay, 21
Château des Charmes Winery
Rosé Sparkling, 23
Kew Vineyards Pinot Meunier
Sparkling, 25
Magnotta Blanc de Noirs
Sparkling Wine, 27
Peller Estates Ice Cuvée
Classic, 29
Stonehouse Vineyard 1793, 127
Sue-Ann Staff Estate Winery Riesling, 55
sweetness
about, 14–15
luscious, 117
sweetness, dry, red wines
Closson Chase Churchside
Pinot Noir, 83
Cloudsley Cellars Pinot Noir, 85
Domaine Queylus Réserve du
Domaine Pinot Noir, 87
EastDell Cabernet Franc, 89
Featherstone Cabernet Franc, 91
Flat Rock Cellars Gravity
Pinot Noir, 93
Henry of Pelham Baco Noir, 95
LOLA Cabernet Sauvignon /
Cabernet Franc, 97
Malivoire Farmstead Gamay, 99
Peller Estates Private Reserve
Cabernet Sauvignon, 101
Peninsula Ridge Estates Winery
Reserve Meritage, 103
Queenston Mile Vineyard
Pinot Noir, 105
Rennie Estate Winery Obsidian
Cabernet Sauvignon, 107
Rosehall Run Cherrywood
Pinot Noir, 109
Rosewood "Night Moves"

Gamay, 111
16 Mile Cellar Rebel Pinot Noir
Gamay, 81
Southbrook Gamay, 113
Trius Estates Red The Icon, 115
sweetness, dry, rosé wines
Mindful Rosé, 69
Paradise Grapevine Vin de Soif
Gamay & Zweigelt, 73
Revel Cider IBI Apollo Rosé, 75
Southbrook Triomphe Cabernet
Franc Rosé, 77
sweetness, dry, sparkling wines
Angels Gate Sparkling
Chardonnay, 21
Château des Charmes Winery
Rosé Sparkling, 23
Kew Vineyards Pinot
Meunier Sparkling, 25
sweetness, dry, white wines
KIN Vineyards Chardonnay, 37
Mindful Pinot Grigio, 39
On Seven the Pursuit
Chardonnay, 41
Oxley Estate Winery
Auxerrois, 43
Paradise Grapevine Golden
Hour, 45
Peninsula Ridge Estates Winery
Sauvignon Blanc, 47
Queenston Mile Vineyard
Chardonnay, 49
Reif Estate Winery Reserve
Pinot Grigio, 51
Rosewood Cellars Legacy
Spiced Mead, 53
Trail Estate Winery
Chardonnay, 57
Twenty Bees Pinot Grigio, 59
Vineland Estates Winery
Chardonnay Musqué, 61
Waupoos Estate Winery
Auxerrois, 63
Wayne Gretzky Estates
Sauvignon Blanc, 65
sweetness, luscious, dessert wines
Château des Charmes
Vidal Icewine, 119
Magnotta Cabernet Franc
Icewine, 123
Reif Estate Winery Vidal
Icewine, 125

sweetness, medium sweet
    Peller Estates Ice Cuvée
        Classic, 29
sweetness, off-dry, rosé wines
    Oxley Estate Winery Cab
        Syrah Rosé, 71
sweetness, off-dry, sparkling wines
    Magnotta Blanc de Noirs
        Sparkling Wine, 27
sweetness, off-dry, white wines
    Cave Spring Riesling, 33
    Flat Rock Cellars Nadja's
        Vineyard Riesling, 35
    Sue-Ann Staff Estate Winery
        Riesling, 55
sweetness, sweet, dessert wines
    Lakeview Cellars Vidal
        Icewine, 121
    Stonehouse Vineyard 1793, 127

T

taste, influences on, 6–7
tasting, aggressive, 7
tasting notes, 6, 7–8, 9
Theise, Terry, 6, 7
touring
    about, 132
    clothing for, 133
    exploring while, 133
    number of visits per day, 134
    protecting wine while, 133
    scent, wearing, 133
    transportation, 132, 133
Trail Estate Winery Chardonnay, 57
Trius Estates Red The Icon, 115
Twenty Bees Pinot Grigio, 59
typicity, 45

V

vidal blanc
    Château des Charmes
        Vidal Icewine, 119
    Lakeview Cellars Vidal
        Icewine, 121
    Reif Estate Winery Vidal
        Icewine, 125
vin de soif, 73
Vineland Estates Winery
    Chardonnay Musqué, 61
vintages, 136

W

Waupoos Estate Winery Auxerrois, 63
Wayne Gretzky Estates
    Sauvignon Blanc, 65
white wines
    about, 31
    Cave Spring Riesling, 33
    Flat Rock Cellars Nadja's
        Vineyard Riesling, 35
    KIN Vineyards Chardonnay, 37
    Mindful Pinot Grigio, 39
    On Seven the Pursuit
        Chardonnay, 41
    Oxley Estate Winery
        Auxerrois, 43
    Paradise Grapevine
        Golden Hour, 45
    Peninsula Ridge Estates Winery
        Sauvignon Blanc, 47
    Queenston Mile Vineyard
        Chardonnay, 49
    Reif Estate Winery Reserve
        Pinot Grigio, 51
    Rosewood Cellars Legacy
        Spiced Mead, 53
    Sue-Ann Staff Estate
        Winery Riesling, 55
    Trail Estate Winery
        Chardonnay, 57
    Twenty Bees Pinot Grigio, 59
    Vineland Estates Winery
        Chardonnay Musqué, 61
    Waupoos Estate Winery
        Auxerrois, 63
    Wayne Gretzky Estates
        Sauvignon Blanc, 65
Whittall, Luke
    about, 4–5, 135
wine, describing
    aromatic descriptors, about, 5,
        8, 15–16
    point scores, 9–11
    tasting notes, 7, 8–9
Wine Aroma Wheel, 8
wine pairing
    about, 16, 73, 129
    with attitude, 129
    with context, 16, 129, 130–131
    with food, 73 (see also food
        pairing, dessert wines; food
        pairing, red wines; food
        pairing, rosé wines; food

wine pairing continued
    pairing, sparkling wines; food
        pairing, white wines)
    with mood, 131
wine regions
    Harrow, 43
    Ottawa, 37
    Prince Edward County, 63
wineries
    Angels Gate Winery, 21
    Cave Spring Vineyard, 33
    Château des Charmes, 23, 119
    Cloudsley Cellars, 85
    Domaine Queylus, 87
    EastDell Estates, 89
    Featherstone Estate Winery &
        Vineyard, 91
    Flat Rock Cellars, 35, 93
    Henry of Pelham Family
        Estate Winery, 95
    Kew Vineyards, 25
    KIN Vineyards, 37
    Lakeview Cellars Estate
        Winery, 121
    Lakeview Wine Co., 39, 69
    Magnotta Winery, 27, 123
    Malvoire Wine Co., 99
    On Seven Estate Winery, 41
    Oxley Estate Winery, 43, 71
    Paradise Grapevine, 45, 73

Pelee Island Winery, 97
Peller Estates, 29, 101
Peninsula Ridge Estates Winery,
    47, 103
Queenston Mile Vineyard, 49, 105
Reif Estate Winery, 51, 125
Rennie Estate Winery, 107
Revel Cider, 75
Rosehall Run Vineyard, 109
Rosewood Estates Winery &
    Meadery, 53
Rosewood Winery, 111
16 Mile Cellar, 81
Southbrook Organic Vineyards,
    77, 113
Stonehouse Vineyard, 125
Sue-Ann Staff Estate Winery, 55
Trail Estate Winery, 57
Trius Winery, 115
Twenty Bees, 59
Vineland Estates Winery, 61
Waupoos Estates Winery, 63
Wayne Gretzky Estates Winery,
    63, 65
wines selected for book, 11–12
wine tasting, protocol for book, 13

Z
zweigelt, Paradise Grapevine Vin de
    Soif Gamay & Zweigelt, 73